THE HINDU JOURNEY

THE HINDU JOURNEY

A Sociological Perspective

Tribhuwan Kapur

GYAN PUBLISHING HOUSE
NEW DELHI-110002

The Hindu Journey : A Sociological Perspective

Rs. 450

ISBN: 81-212-0835-1

Published in 2003 in India by
Gyan Publishing House
5, Ansari Road, Darya Ganj, New Delhi-110002
Phones : 23282060, 23261060, Fax : 011-23285914
E-mail : gyanbook@vsnl.com
Website : http://www.gyanbooks.com

Laser Typesetting at : Shree Vaishnavi Creations, Delhi
Printed at : Mehra Offset Press

DEDICATION

To all those who have inspired
me to take up this journey.

Contents

Preface

This is an ethnographic record that covers more that two decades of endeavor in attempting to learn theoretically, and then to put into practice, the forest teachings of the Eternal religion. Being both theoretical and practical means simply that it is a record of the conversations that I had with some knowledgeable sources from the 1970s onwards when my interest in spirituality become very intense and could not be contained simply by reading books about the spiritual experience. I wanted to experience it first hand and then talk to sources who were genuinely spiritual no matter what their outward presentation of self. Indeed the spiritual experiences that came my way over these years could easily be wished away as induced by hypnosis, or due to my own imagination, but then why would they have persisted even when the sages and yogis in whose presence I had them were no longer there.?

Tribhuwan Kapur

PART ONE

The Forest Teachings

It became obvious to me as the years went by that spiritual experience, or its counterpart the mystical experience, are such that they cannot be scrutinized under a microscope and in fact even if this could be done at some future point in civilizations, it would best be avoided. This is because everything that is sacred would be profaned. I recall for example the ability I developed very gradually to be able to experience a very subtle flow of light around a person or a tree with open eyes. It is a very subtle light, like a fine mist that surrounds a person. Contrary to reports that I studied on this phenomena, the flow of light that I witnessed had the shape of the human body itself stretching out about a foot around it and being the 'brightest' around the head and shoulders. The light mist would begin pulsating and gradually the person would still be there but very faintly and glowing golden yellow. I give this example at the onset because it seems to me that reports other than this one posit that the light around the human body, a kind of energy field, is like a ball or an egg and stretches out several feet in all directions. This was certainly not my experience.

The point I want to make is that these phenomena have a certain physiological basis, that is quite clear. However, it is also very obvious that such sacred experiences should not be explained biologically and by the theories of physicists. In providing such explanations it would only be too clear that the sacred would be trampled upon mercilessly making spirituality an aberration and science an abomination. Whatever the intermesh science and spirituality must keep to their territory in the main if we are not to destroy both of them with our intellect. Therefore I have refrained from trying to give explanations of the spiritual experiences I have had. Further I must point out that the spiritual experience is not something to shout about. The spiritual experiences that came my way, almost as a routine, were quiet and dignified. But some of them were made into pedestrian affairs by one or more of my companions who I related them to: they talked of these experiences as biological or physiological in origin and thus we parted ways.

Before we go further a word about the background to these conversations encounters and experiences: I was always inclined towards spirituality and the supernatural and even while in school I devoured all that I could get in this field, mainly autobiographies and occult literature.

I was certainly not among the non-believers or cynics. Indeed I believed that the phenomena described could definitely happen and that it would not serve any purpose for anyone to invent stories to entertain people or to try and make money. As for myself my interest in studying mystic and occult literature developed into later life and I read with avid fascination the stories of adventurers of the spirit. By this time I had met Sri Turiya and was in the thick of spiritual experiences myself and could relate to the adventures of others much better. I could collate and compare their statements to what I was experiencing and felt definite that there was a world(s) that I was exploring which others in the same field had not published about much. This is the world of 'gazing' into other dimensions.

Gazing is done best on a night when there is a full moon. A comfortable and safe (from insects and animals) perch is required for this activity. Once the proper steps are taken a new world suddenly opens up and the person who is gazing (the gazer) begins to witness the dance of creation. Subtle images begin to emerge from anything that he gazes upon and these in themselves acquire volition. Very soon a full scale movement of images of humans and non-humans begins to enthrall and mesmerize the gazer. Time has no meaning at all and there is no feeling that one is running out of time and should stop gazing. Thus I have gazed from midnight to sunrise without feeling the slightest sense of boredom. The point however is that the images in motion that one gazes upon provide one an ingress into the philosophy of the Eternal Religion. And are an entry point into matters pertaining to the heart of religion, and more especially the religions and spirituality of India. I will have more to say about gazing at a later stage, but I have bought this up because it is one of the most important ways to gain knowledge of spiritualism of India first hand. Further I would say that most serious, that is thinking human beings, have had an occasional brush with gazing at some point of time or the other. However since this takes place without guidance or without any theoretical expectation, the experience is enjoyed, but is then pushed away since it has nobody to explain or corroborate it. Gazing is the entrance into almost any topic of one's choice of study. The topic itself is to be held in the mind as one gazes into the trees and shrubs, into the light and shadow. What then suddenly begins to happen is exhilarating stunning and interesting beyond belief. Yet there is a bugbear. If the person concerned who is gazing is not spiritually evolved to some basic degree, and has intentions other than spiritual, gazing can lead to the loss of life, property and cause damage to mental health. That is why gazing remains a mystery even though it is accessible to almost anyone who is capable of sparing time to do it.

I have brought up this matter of gazing because this is and was one of the techniques of meditation that Sri Turiya taught me in simple words and let me go into the intricacies of the meditation. In fact the discussions on Hinduism that I had with him were based very largely on what I had experienced while gazing at clusters of trees, shrubs, rock faces and even the wall of a room. There was no shadow of doubt in my mind that since my interest was in Indian spirituality, many scenes appropriate to this religion would unfold right before my open eyes and I would see the play of the spirit in all its glory. Here I want to add a qualification, which I find that my colleagues fail to do—what I was gazing at was a subtle interplay of images, so subtle and real that one could watch it for hours without getting exhausted. They were not like celluloid images which are very hard and harsh and literally splash colour into the viewer. The images of the gazer are subtle and soft and incredibly tantalizing. Very soon the gazer is tantalized and mesmerized into seeing the images play out a message in incredible ways.

Yes, it has to be pointed out that to see these images in all their glory and subtlety there has to be a different state of mind induced by meditation or chanting during the day or else nothing will manifest. The entrance to the world of the gazer is a spiritual life and the specifics include the raising of consciousness by meditation and spiritual cleansing.

Without the beneficial input of a relatively simple and uncomplicated life, inwardly and outwardly, gazing cannot be carried on for any length of time. Moreover the experience can be nerve wracking and injurious to the mental health of the person who tries to enter into this field of endeavour in a cavalier fashion. In my case

Sri Turiya, after some initial instructions used to discuss with me only what I had seen in my gazing practices and this meant that the topic of conversation had to be decided by looking into the dimly lit world of the jungle, or the shimmering patterns on a screen or wall till the patterns turned into images and a gazing session began. For me gazing was a regular activity when I was with Sri Turiya, or out of Delhi on a vacation. However unless I had my mind off immediate necessities like food and shelter I was usually not able to muster up even the motive to start gazing. If I did try to gaze under conditions of stress physically and mentally the images would not come and the gazing would not be gazing at all. Rather it was just watching the play of light and shadow, a play which did not have the free volition of gazing.

It has to be pointed out that I had a background on Indian spiritualism and had read voraciously some of the popular literature on the subject. As such I was able to identify the topic which was to be meditated upon and discussed with Sri Turiya, on my next contact with him. I would also like to add that my interaction with Sri Turiya at his mountain retreat tended to be quite brief but intense. I would go there and after a few pleasantries the conversation would take a spiritual turn and I would discuss to my heart's content the topics that had come up to me during my gazing sessions. Sri Turiya was not particularly interested in the entirety of my gazing, and had remarked quite often that gazing is only the means for the topic it creates to become alive and interesting. Being full of imagery a 'dry' topic is given a context which is mysterious, paradoxical or even horrific. As such gazing is not an end in itself but a means to opening the door to further discussion. It also imparts the discussion an immediacy that mere discussion cannot have. That is why Sri Turiya regarded gazing as basic to the experience of spirituality, but this experience was nevertheless limited by the extent of the talent of the person concerned. Thus Sri Turiya had pointed out time and again that the gazing that an aspirant does is determined by his nature. If the person is of a creative and imaginative bent his gazing is truly tremendous taking him out of this world into many new dimensions. It could become so fascinating that the aspirant loses track of the main purpose of gazing itself which is to isolate topics for clarification and discussion. Thus Sri Turiya pointed out that in ages past right down to the present times a vast majority of would be sadhus and yogis ended up seeing tantalizing fantasies and picture shows without following them up with any discussion or analysis which would clarify spiritual precepts to them.

I have tried to stress the role of gazing from the outset for I believe this is one of the spiritual activities which can benefit any aspirant. As Sri Turiya pointed out to me that it takes only the will to arrange the situation that one can look out in a relaxed way on a pattern of soft light and shade, in the open or inside a room. As one looks on in a relaxed manner a picture play begins, and it is here that most of the aspirants begin to flounder. They start to get too excited and get hyper resulting in the images disappearing. Thus though gazing can be experienced to be a reality, for it to become wholly viable a modicum of detachment and discipline over the emotions is a necessity. So gazing is a type of meditation in itself and does not call for any preconceptions, or the need to conjure up any shapes. By experiments it becomes clear that a certain type of posture, silence, and a body that is comfortable is all that is required for it.

Gazing has been until the present times a jealously guarded secret and I asked Sri Turiya if I should mentain it at all in my ethnographic account. He was of the view that the 'real thing' ought to be maintained amidst a plethora of endless meditations which in his view did not have the dynamic value of gazing, and could not be experienced in so graphic a manner. I realize myself that what he said has substance in it because having gazed into the beyond on several occasions I realize that it is not an entertainment at all, but a serious spiritual activity. The drawback as it were of gazing is that it has to be thought or talked about to make sense. This requires that one talks about spiritual matters with an adept, or at least get into the conversational meditation with the subject of gazing held in the mind. In other words for gazing to be fully utilized the pictures and sequences that it has engendered should be resuscitated again in the mind during conventional sit down meditation or Dhyan.

I would like to stress this point again, since it is a key point in the forest teachings of Sri Turiya and was stressed upon me many times in my years of association with him. There are at least two components in the spiritual process: one is simply gazing and logging up an archive of images and image sequences; the other is to sit down comfortably and review these images or picture sequences. If one is fortunate one then has something to talk about with the preceptor instead of going to him without anything in particular in his mind. This 'empty minded' approach to spirituality was extremely distasteful to Sri Turiya and he would often make fun of the people who expected something to be filled into their intellect and make no effort whatsoever to comprehend. Such people were regarded by Sri Turiya as people who just want to be part of a propaganda machine but do nothing creative in the world of spirituality. He was however sympathetic towards them and said in due course of time their effort would by themselves make a good climate for them to gaze, meditate and discuss spiritual matters.

Most of my interactions with Sri Turiya were in his northern Indian hill retreat, but later significant ones were held in Delhi which he visited occasionally for various purposes. However we did have quite a few roving conversations when we went for an evening walk, or strolled in the moonlight towards a distant peak to watch the sunrise from there. However late night sessions also generated a lot of data for me, as did the after breakfast coffee interactions. Almost all the conversations were in English, a language which Sri Turiya spoke most of the time. He was not a native of the town in which he had settled some forty years back, and hailed from the plains of Uttar Pradesh. As such the spiritual knowledge that he imparted was not ethnic in content but pertained to spirituality in general. Again though Sri Turiya did have visitors including local ones I did not have much insight into whether these were casual visitors or they were aspirants. My feeling was that these people came to have a word with him, and exchange a few notes by way of the latest views and news in the town which was some miles down south. I was aware that there were other committed disciples that he had, and one of them had built a small hut near the main retreat and another one had built a regular house some way down the slope from the main retreat.

I was in no position in the early days of my association with Sri Turiya to be of any financial benefit to him. As it is I stayed in the lower storey of his two storey retreat as a guest. This was not my privilege alone as he had guests or 'friends' the whole year round. Thus the picture of conversations and discussions which I am presenting is not one of a spokesman for a large body of disciples. It is a picture that fits my experiences with him, and being academically inclined I must point out that most of the other people who came there were of the Bhakti orientation in which emotional and spiritual love is used to generate peace tranquility, bliss and love. I am not against the bhakti path of realization and in fact this path has been held by the bhakti saints like Kabir as the most appropriate for the Kal Yug, which is the present Age of Degeneration, in which only the surface courtesies survive, and underneath these there are tremendous hostilities, enmities, bitterness and hatred.

I found however that the vedantic method of inquiring dispassionately and objectively about the spirit was much closer to my bent of mind than the emotionality of bhakti yoga. As such my training over the few decades that I knew Sri Turiya meant that he had to specially make an effort to put into words experiences and concepts that normally go unexplained, are not discussed, and it is assumed to everyone is agreed about their usage.

The exposition which follows is an ethnographic record concerning the conversations that I had with Sri Turiya over a long period of time. However there were also long periods of time when I did not see him at all since I was busy with my studies. However towards the end of the discipleship I had the opportunity to spend a relatively longer period of time with him and was therefore able to wind up my first phase with him. The second phase was to recollect and meditate on the concepts and experiences that I had when I was with him. The record that I am presenting is not a linear one but is textured like a fabric and many of the themes are interwoven and weave in and out of other concepts. The spirituality under discussion is the Eternal Religion or Spirituality, or the Sanatan Dharma. So it is not a religion that we will be going into in terms of specific ethnic rituals and chants but the very root of spirituality— a spirituality that has no traceable beginning and no foreseeable end because it does not depend on human bodies to exist. It has everything to do with the human spirit, both individual and collective, not only in this world but also in the hereafter.

The second phase with Sri Turiya was a great challenge to me because when I went to meet him after a gap of an year he told me that since I had time on my hand I should go and stay in a hut in the mountains and manage my own affairs. He felt that this was absolutely necessary for my spiritual maturing. It was a deadly challenge for me as I was doing my doctorate then and had to gather some information about rites and rituals in that area. In fact my research required that I go native, and interact with the people there and visit their rituals, talk to them about their interpretation of why they were doing what they were doing. I had already put by money for my expedition in postdated cheques, and Sri Turiya's challenge thrilled me. It put me in a state of panic and expectation and I remember literally sweating when he proposed this to me. However Sri Turiya was a gentle teacher and he pointed out to me that I could have a hut at reasonable rent just a few miles uphill, and that I could come and meet him, now and then, and the discussions could go on. I was however in a different state of mind. Somewhere within me I knew that the further I stayed from Sri Turiya the better it would be for me. It had come to the point that my academic conversations were beginning to take a turn that was not palatable to Sri Turiya. He was getting on in the years and he definitely preferred to emote spiritually with his several other disciples rather than split hairs with me.

I was very hesitant about where to go but one other disciple who was there at the same time told me I could go further north towards a village which was very scenic. I decided to give it a try and went there by bus. At this time I had a very bad back and the slightest movement gave me shooting pains and to this day I do not know how I completed that journey, on a road that wound in and out of the mountains. Even today that series of moments are clear as crystal in my mind. However it was as if a higher power was cradling me and keeping me safe and preventing me from making a spectacle of myself, by shouting or bursting into tears.

It was in this village that I met a remarkable man, who was mystery even to those who lived close to him. It was as if the very power which was looking after me put me immediately in touch with this man. I had gone around the village and spent one night in the open with my baggage, when I was told that I should contact Kaptan Saab, a landowner in that area, as someone who would be able to get me a one-room accommodation. I walked through the village road with its few shops until I was at the shop of the general merchant.

'Where can I meet Kaptan Saab?, I asked an old man wearing a worn suit, and a crew cut.

'Why do you want to meet him?' he asked.

'I want a room to live in, in this village'. I told him politely

'Come with me', said the man confidently.

This was my meeting with my second teacher, who was a master much more hidden than Sri Turiya.

However in this I do intend to go linearly, in that I will first deal with the teachings of Sri Turiya and then describe my experiences with Kaptan Saab, and the training I had under him. The two men were totally different, and while Sri Turiya still had the aura of a 'spiritual' person given to such 'holy' pursuits, I found that Kaptan Saab was in fact totally free of any frills. He had perfected the role of an ordinary person, but he was a totally practical person.

So I will now start my account of the conversations with Sri Turiya, and once they are completed, or at least adequately delineated I will go onto the spiritual adventures I had with Kaptan Saab. This will then put me in a position to compare the two kinds of spiritual knowledge that I had the opportunity to encounter in the field I do want to emphasize there is nothing ethnic in this account because Kaptan Saab was himself an immigrant from the plains and had settled in the village area where I kept my headquarters for my studies.

I recall that evening and night in 1977 very well. It was the month of June and I had been doing my gazing practices for about five years with the help of a candle and some still water in a shallow basin. The practice was to gaze at the flame of the candle until the mind quieted down. So far as the water was concerned the practice was to look into the water when it was still and to see into the shadow areas and the lighted areas. I found that with practice both the practices created visual extrapolations. Sometimes when I gazed at the candle flame some ten feet in front of me I could see faint reflections of towers and aerial highways. At times I could see entire sequences of subtle image plays which had sequential messages. So also in the still water of the basin. As I would gaze on it new shapes and forms beyond my imagination would appear and there were times I had to halt the practice when there was a fear that these shapes might actually materialize beside me, so threatening was their reality.

One evening when I was doing gazing on the candle flame I realized that it's brief flickering was creating a shadow play on the curtains and wall behind it. I watched bewitched by the images for over an hour. All across my field of vision people of all ages lay sprawled out sleeping. They were still wearing their working clothes but they were asleep and obviously dreaming. Every now and then one of them would slowly turn over or give a groan of satisfaction. It was an entire world that was asleep and inert. As I watched in fascination there was a sudden movement and beyond a hedge that separated the sleepers and the other part of the room I saw an unimaginably beautiful woman dressed in a green lahnga and a green top. She was fair and flawless. The vision lasted a bare few seconds and with a shimmer of bangles she was gone. I spent the rest of my vigil hoping she would arrive but she did not, and I was left with a tantalizing view of the easily the most beautiful woman I had ever seen, dreaming or awake.

I was somewhat well versed with Indian philosophy by then having done eclectic reading on the subject and it did not take me long to realize that the vision I had was that of Maya, the veil of illusion, and the woman that represented Maya in this vision was the incredibly beautiful young woman. Yet when I tried I realized that there was hardly anything in the literature on Maya beyond a few pithy sentences. That is why that June evening I wanted to ask Sri Turiya about Maya, the veil of illusion and what it was all about. The many pundits and yogi's with whom I had tried to raise the topic seemed quite ignorant about it, even trying to dismiss it as of no consequence. My position was that if Sri Turiya was himself unable to deliver the message then I would be left alone trying to get over the bewildering and mesmeric effect that the vision of Maya had had on me.

We were sitting on his balcony, drinking tea, when I raised the question.

'Sri Turiya, I have been trying to get myself extricated from the image of a dream woman I saw in one of my gazing visions where I saw the world asleep and dreaming, and Maya the temptress, or the woman of illusion coming and tending to them, delighted that they were asleep. Seconds after I saw that vision I realized that this was the power that was called Maya, and that it was a feminine power that held sway over most of the world. I have tried to read about this power and to talk to various people about it in a covert sometimes casual way but beyond talk of the 'web of Illusion' and it's dangers I have got nothing substantial. Nevertheless Maya is obviously a very important power since it puts and keeps mankind sleeping and dreaming of great things. By the time they think that they should wake up it is already too late for them to do anything and they bemoan their fate. They were dreaming of doing things and passed their life in sleep but were unable to see that the illusions they harbored both at night and while 'awake' during the daytime were very often wholly worthless, and their lives had gone waste. 'Doesn't this make Maya one of the most powerful forces operating in the world?' I asked Sri Turiya rhetorically.

'I knew that you would one day come across this barrier, and to tell you the truth this is the only real information I have that you have been assiduously doing your gazing. Yes Maya is the power that keeps the world happily asleep and prevents human beings from looking into reality.' Sri Turiya stared pensively at his glass of tea. I did not think that this was enough clarification. 'How do you mean?' I asked wanting him to talk at length on a topic that had bothered me for months on end and had even entered into my subconscious dreaming mind.

'This is the power of the feminine forces, which are the real challenge. Before a yogi can comprehend what is love he has to get over the sensuality of Maya, who is beauty personified. Believe me when I tell you that I know what you mean. When I saw Maya I was older than you and my mind went into orbit. Wherever I looked I saw her form, and her beauty. Like you I felt half mad and half crazy. I became desperate in my gazing routines trying to get a glimpse of her, and I did! But never for long enough. Even now when sometimes I am walking alone on the mountain side sometimes I feel her presence in the forest and I am so sure she is there that I stop and scan the whole area. Believe it or not there have been times when she has given me a glimpse of herself as a peasant woman of incredible grace and beauty.' Sri Turiya stopped.

'What do you make of it all, after all who is she, what is her history, who is her mate, to which of the powers of the universe is she allied, what are her properties and powers – do tell me Sri Turiya, I am very keen to know, indeed tantalized by this form and power. I have myself started getting lost in hallucinations and I see her everywhere, in hidden places, in parks and in parties. I can catch a glimpse of her but rarely is it possible to talk to her. I humbly request you, Sri Turiya, that if you won't talk to me about her, tell me then how do I talk to her, face to face!' I was in a state of excitement and panic. The tantalizing form of Maya had completely possessed me and made all that I did difficult in the extreme. In fact I sometimes had the feeling in the mountains that I might walk over a precipice in my preoccupied state of mind. In the metropolitan I feared for my safety on the road. One of my friends had been run over by a truck and in the state I was in I was sure that something terrible was going to happen to me also.

'I can see you have a problem' 'said Sri Turiya thoughtfully, 'but their is no easy solution!'

Anything would be better than this state of distraction', I said in agitation.

'You would have to exert yourself, quite a bit', said Sri Turiya pensively.

'I am willing to go to my limits', I said defiantly.

'I can't talk to you about Maya. Only she can tell you what you want to know. It isn't as if I don't know the theories, but these are very brief. Moreover even to talk of Maya is to put oneself under her spell. That is why you will find that there are very few references to Maya in our scriptures. This is despite the fact that Maya is a supremely potent teacher of both matter and spirit. But you are already under her spell, and I can see a glazed look in your eye.......... It's possible if you can see her and talk to her you would at least have a further reason to be circumambulated.' Sri Turiya was deliberately giving me time to think and decide.

'It's all right,' I said, 'I'm willing to go through whatever you want me to do.......... my present condition of stupefaction is getting to be beyond my endurance. It was not as if I could not carry on the normal tasks of living. It was just that there was a terrible absent mindedness in my head, which did not seem to go away. And when I was having a quiet moment, it would be disturbed by visions of that beautiful woman, I had seen while gazing.

'There is a temple about three hours from here. Two hours by bus and another hour by bridle path. The temple is deserted except for a priest who controls access to its main worship room. You will have to go there and get the key to the room from the priest. He will readily give it to you provided you are willing to go through the mandatory prayers to the deity. After that you can sit there and gaze at the lamps that shine on even during the day. I think that the night time would be the best and that you should be able to shake off this fuzziness that you are experiencing constantly. There is however one warning I would like to give you.......... when Maya appears before you, as she must in that temple, kindly don't forget that she is an ultimately potent abstract force which has millions of people entrapped in their dreams of grandeur. She is wholly adept at making slaves of her devotees and you seem to be well on your way in becoming one of these. Do remember however that your purpose is not to have dreams and illusions but to be in naked touch with reality. As such you must not address her as you would normally an extraordinarily beautiful woman. You must address her as a powerful deity, which she is. Try to forget her beauty –it is just a trap. Imagine if you can that an old lady is appearing before you gaze. Use any subterfuge you can to remind yourself that your purpose to ask her questions about illusion and reality—that's all. Don't think she has time to materialize herself and to be your personal friend. Maya has no personal friend, she is an individuated deity. Her appearing before you as you gazed is not fun for her. She is held up because she must answer a few questions to you before she moves on and plays –Maya loves to play and you are coming in her way ...'

Briefly Sri Turiya gave me instructions how to get to the temple and told me that I should leave without further delay. He seemed agitated and explained that the very mention of the word Maya was enough to make him feel like meditation since he himself in his younger days had something to do with her. It had not been a pleasant experience and this was one of the reasons he himself did not want to talk too much about her.

I packed a small haversack and left for the temple. My plan was to reach it just as it was getting dark, have the prayer said and immediately being gazing into the lamp with the right type of flame.

I was shivering in anticipation, and the thought did occur to my mind that I was getting myself involved in something I had hardly anticipated. On the other hand my passion for knowing about that lady that I had seen in my gazing overrode all my caution. When I was riding in the bus I had in fact begun literally enjoying myself as if I was going out on a picnic and the thought did not strike me that I might be opening myself out to supernatural forces that could take over my life.

All the while I had convinced my self that I was not

dabbling in black practices and that the deities that I was involved with were the white force. That is to say the local deities of the area were not my concern – it was the deities of the vedic pantheon that were my area of interest and study. The bus rolled on and lulled me into a state of confidence, indeed rashness. Soon I began to feel that I was going to meet a cherished friend and the anticipation excited me. Strangely I never did consider that I could have been going to my doom and that whatever force that were unleased by my gazing the lamps in that temple, might turn out to be inimical to me, both mentally and physically.

The ramshackle bus dropped me off at roadside near a small tea stall. On the pretext of having a glass of tea I enquired about the path to the temple. The wizened man gave me some directions and told me to leave quickly if I wanted to get there before dark. He also told me there were no tourist hotels, or places to stay at night. I told him that I knew somebody in the nearby village. I paid for the tea and left by the steeply inclining path towards the temple. The sun was still up and as I climbed the atmosphere started cooling down making my sweat feel cool on my brow. My mind was relaxed and alert. Apart from my covert agenda of gazing I was also interested in seeing the temple itself. Sri Turiya had mentioned that it was a beautiful temple and I was looking forward to seeing the frescoes and statues. The sky was a deep blue and the steady cool breeze made the upward inclines easy to walk. I walked steadily and before I knew it I had reached the crest of the hill and could see the pillars of the temple. They reminded of the coliseum in a miniature sort of way and of temples that one sees in the south of India. As I approached the entrance which was walled over with a carved wall, a man with diacritical marks of a priest approached me. I greeted him with folded hands, as is the custom and gave my name. I told him I wanted a prayer performed and wanted to spend the night in prayer inside with the statues of the gods. I could tell he found me a little peculiar, but then it was obvious that ordinarily a person would not come to this temple without a purpose.

The prayer the priest said took me into the late evening, after which I ate some biscuits from my haversack in the courtyard. I went and drank some water from the spring some way beyond the temple. By the time I was back the priest had refilled the oil lamps and had arranged a rug on which the aspirant could sit and pray. He left with the word that the storm clouds were building up to the east. He pointed out that should they rain I should bolt the temple door from the inside otherwise the area within might gather water.

As soon as the priest had left I went and sat on the rug and quieted my mind. At first the unusual surroundings made focusing my mind on the largest flame near a large idol extremely difficult. However I persisted with my gazing, and images began to flow. My impatience was itself a problem as each time my gazing began to show results the flow of images was disrupted since gazing demands a completely relaxed attitude, and I was very excited. It was the first time that I was gazing alone within the precincts of a temple. I could hear the roll of the thunder outside and this added to my distraction. Finally I was able to settle down and immerse myself in my gazing. Suddenly the earlier sequence of sleepers began to take life and while I was still trying to wonder what it meant I saw an exquisitely enchanting woman sitting near the main idol in the temple. She wore a green silk sari with a ochre coloured jacket. Her hair was jet black and I could see that she was smiling at me.

Once again I found that my heart was thumping against my ribcage and that my throat was choking. I could not say a word and kept staring at her my forehead beaded with sweat.

I took a swig of water from the flask I had with me and felt much better, and tried to cool myself with deep breaths. I was almost sure that the woman I knew was the personification of Maya would soon vanish leaving me distraught and in disarray. 'Please don't go, I said in a deep gruff voice that was hoarse with emotion.

'You have been seeking a meeting with me... go-ahead ! What do you want to know?' she said. Her voice was like the rustling of silk and reminded me of the song of some rare bird as it had a warbling effect.

'You can ask me anything you like, but don't take too long. It is injurious to be in my company for human beings, as they tend to get obsessed with my image. Asked me anything you like and then let me go............ I have things to do, and you are holding me up' Her voice was sweet and her tone was polite. But it was obvious that she meant business.

'How come the forest teachings have hardly a mention of you. Why do the Upanishads tend to avoid mentioning Maya and her role in creation?' I was burning with curiosity.

'There was the oral tradition of the Vedas that was put into script... but there were huge chunks of knowledge that were not scripted and allowed to remain as areas that could be reached through meditation, by the aspirants and the seers who are aware of this. The power of illusion, an original and feminine power that goes by the name Maya, remainded in that part of the oral tradition that was not noted down into the forest teachings'. She smiled sweetly showing a row of teeth which were like pearls. I remembered what Sri Turiya had said about not being distracted by here form and it was with difficulty that I kept my mind on the conversation.

'What were the criteria for putting some knowledge in writing and leaving out the rest?' I asked.

'The criteria of leaving out large chunks of the oral tradition from the areas that were put into script was simply that there would be a second phase in the Eternal Religion when this would be done.' Maya looked like a petulant child.

'Who would do this ...... and who would believe in it? Are you telling me you are inaugurating the second phase or the new phase of the Eternal Religion?' I was incredulous.

'I think you lack the basic idea of the oral tradition in the Eternal Religion. These were not the work of some single seer. Dozens of seers worked on kernels of truth that were discovered by the yogi's of old. Only then were they put together into the scripts. I am talking about the forest teachings. Yes when I appear in this form to you I am telling you that some of these conversations will stir the mind of others and in due course of time a new phase of spirituality will arise...... and you will benefit spiritually. You will gather good karma one day when you tell others of this meeting with me. I will meet others too and they too will confirm what you will put down on paper and in this way gradually an area which has remained in the dark will come out in the open. Contrary to imagination man will aspire more and more to attain spirituality and you yourself will not be able to suppress this meeting with me in this temple. One day, despite your will and your intentions you will describe our meeting. Those who are spiritually inclined will believe and benefit from it'. She smiled again. I found her irresistible in that slight frame which could not have been more than eighteen years of age. Her smile was contagious and she smiled a lot, which was fortunate because it relaxed me. Yet on the inside I was only too aware that a laser like pressure emanated from her eyes.

I knew I had little time with her and that she might never appear in front of me as a result of my gazing.

'Tell me then who are you', I asked finally gaining some control over my faculties.

'I am Maya, the first born of Brahman, and given the responsibility of making all creation. I am Maya the Mother of Creation. I am the source of all gods, big or small and of all created things. They have all come out of myself. If there was a Maya uanished this is what it would deal with. Further all creatures, no matter who or what, must return to me and only then would they be allowed to go back into Brahman. I am the flimsy wall between Truth and Falsehood. I am the Ultimate Power which decides who attains moksa and who wanders on in samsara'. Maya arranged her green silk sari and blushed. 'Doesn't it look as if I am blowing my own trumpet? Singing my own praises? Making tall claims?'

Indeed once she mentioned it I could not help feeling that I had taken leave of my senses.

'You are right, it seems difficult to believe what you are saying...... but you need not be saying anything at all. It is I who is asking you questions......... it is not as if you are praising yourself, you are indeed the ideal mother... you are beautiful beyond description and it is only the form you have come to me that is the source of confusion. If you had donned the mantle of an old woman such words might have been very easily understood'. I stopped flushed with indignation, realizing I was defending her like a lover.

'Don't worry! Carry on with you investigation!' Her voice was imperative.

'How did you create all worlds, all gods, and all beings? Please explain!' I asked placidly.

'I thought, and from the power of my thought, my

cogitation, everything appeared......... this entire Universe, the Cosmos, human beings, beasts, the works... all in the flash of an eye... do you believe what I am saying or do you think you're talking to someone who has taken leave of her senses... you see once Brahman the Ultimate Father had birthed me, he told me that I should paint a pretty picture. So I took buckets of paint and threw them out from the void that Brahman is and when they settled there was a picture... it was pretty in parts and horrific in others. It was too late by then, the deed had been done. The picture came alive and so had life on earth!' She paused awhile looking out of the temple gate which was partially open. The thunderstorm had started and huge drops of rain were falling. I could hear this but I dared not to take my eyes off from Maya. I was desperate to hear anything she said, even if it appeared that she was being flippant or joking. I would have enough time to think all that over later. The priest had told me to shut the door if it rained or the inside of the temple would become flooded. I wanted to comply with that request, but Maya might vanish without a trace, and I would be confused for life!

Without a further thought I eased myself up from the rug and limped across to close the door. It was a heavy wooden door with two partitions and creaked shut. With the door shut I realized that the temple resembled almost an echo chamber. I turned around wondering if she was still there. She was still there but it seemed to me that I had not really seen her before. She looked bewitching and completely at ease with herself. I thought that if there was one person I had seen in my life who was beautiful from without and within it was Maya.

'Madam', I said, 'I have never seen anyone so bewitching as you.......... I just don't want to miss the opportunity of telling you this, although this may be strictly out of place.'

'It is not out of place', said Maya, 'If one wants to awaken a deity one must have a divine love for that deity. I showed myself to you for a few seconds and you have thought of me since then. It is your obsessive condition that forced me to appear before you. You see that is the basic premise of my teaching... it is love that awakens the spirit and the deity is able to help when he or she feels his or her love like a physical lance pushing in towards the chest. Oh, yes sir, I knew you love me to distraction!' She blew a blessing towards me throwing one of the flowers near the idols of the gods. It landed precisely on my head making me laugh. Suddenly I was on a roller coaster laughing as I had never laughed before. With those ripples of laughter in the midst of a huge thunderstorm my spirit was deeply cleansed.

I was feeling dizzy by the time I stopped laughing and got a grip on myself. Maya looked upon me in a bemused way, and I grinned sheepishly.

'I'm sorry', I said, 'I couldn't help myself. I hope you'll excuse me.'

'It's all right', she said, 'sometimes one laughs when he catches the tip of the truth.'

'I realized when I' laughed that if one is really very powerful, indeed all pervading, as you are, then that person is in many ways quite harmless. I feel that you yourself, although perpetration of a billion fantasies, are in fact not at all vindictive, nor do you judge people by their failure to see through to reality. I realize that to you the important aspect is that the divine play must go on. It is none of your concern whether any particular person loses or wins.' I stopped waiting for her comments.

'Everyone comes with his baggages of karma, which have to be played out. If the script is already written, as it is, then the important point is to do one's best, even if defeat is assured. This is one of the facts that have been discussed very briefly in the forest teachings, and they are also reflected much later in the Bhagavad Gita. It is man's fate that a person is born to experience. In the portions of the oral tradition which remains inscribed till today, fate has been emphasized to an extreme degree. Perhaps the Rishi's of old felt that if fate and predestination were put into the scriptural tradition, people might lose interest in trying to make the best of each situation. This would mean, of course, that they were giving a wrong interpretation to the oral tradition on fate'. She made a gesture of helplessness.

'Do you mean to say that there is no degree of freedom for man...... That he has to bow down to his karma and fate and cannot overcome his circumstances on his own? Is it not a fact that we can control our destiny to some extent? I mean I can lift my hands, or sing a song, or go to some place that I like...... all on my own volition, and there will be no power on earth that can stop me doing what I want'.

'What you are saying is that you can do whatever you want. The ancients who preserved the oral tradition in the subcontinent were in fact sages who believed in the complete supremacy of fate, destiny, kismet.............. but when it came to putting it all down in a visual script they stepped back. You see it can be terribly demoralizing to be told to believe that your life is controlled by extraneous powers and forces that will not allow you to do, or say, a single word that is not already written in your stars, so to speak. Thus in many a way the still unscripted oral tradition remains a secret area which can be revealed in toto only at a time when mankind is willing to accept these truths. Man's feeling that he is free, has been planted there by me so as to give him hope amidst hopelessness, and allow him to fight his fate, because the whole of existence is about challenging one's fate boldly and without fear. It is a paradox that the man or woman who in diligently confronts his or her fate is in fact able to break the barrier of illusion, and the veil of mist blows aside. The more that fate is confronted the greater is the certainty that it cannot be changed. However when we talk of fate in the oral tradition of Eternal Religion, we are really talking of the physical configuration, and not facts of the mind. Man is free within his spirit and mind and this freedom comes when the outside situation, no matter what, fails to distract or intimidate him. He becomes immune to the external situation, and within himself he rejoices that he is happy and content despite the walls that imprison him and force him to face different, and often difficult situations. If man truly confronts his life circumstances intelligently then his mind starts looking at reality, face to face, and is able to realize that fate is not the issue at all, the issue is freedom. Freedom itself is inward, something in the configuration of consciousness, within the mind. Yes! Even I can only applaud such a noble soul who is free within and confronting his fate on the outside, that is in the events of his life.' Maya changed her position as the roof of the ancient temple had started dripping at some places. The thunderstorm, and the rolling of thunder still persisted, but the thick stone walls of the temple made it appear as if it were just a seasonal shower. She looked for a place where the drops of water were not falling. She moved away from the oil wick lamps and I saw that she was lit up from within. It was as if she was made of some translucent substance that had a diffused light source inside it. Her face glowed in the darkness and gave it a golden hue, which was also evident on her hands and feet.

'In effect what you are saying is that man can be free of his fate if his attitude changes. Are you saying that man must deal with his life without fear of failure or expectation of reward? But then that is the position the Sri Krishna takes in the Bhagavad Gita... to work without expectation or desire for rewards, or even the hope for recognition. If man is able to do that he is a sage, a rishi, a yogi, an enlightened and self realized soul. He has conquered the oppressive forces of his fate and his consciousness reigns supreme. He becomes, so to speak a hidden master, a person contributing to the moral and spiritual upkeep of the world.' I wanted to go on with my observations but I was extremely wary of Maya's presence. The time was past midnight and I was certainly not taking her for granted. But a doubt had started creeping up on me, and I didn't want it to spoil my concentration, so I voiced it aloud.

'Mahamaya, I'm extremely embarrassed to ask you this question, but how do I really know that you are Maya... not an extremely intelligent woman from the world of Spirits?'

'You are not expected to believe in me... go by the logic of my words, and how helpful they are to you. You have been very keen to have someone, anyone, elaborate the nature of the veil of illusion, or the mists of time which shroud reality. It is because of your long standing meditation and desire to meet me that you are here in this temple sitting with me. Come here and touch my hand, I am real! I am much more real that the rest of humanity put together. Mankind dances to my tune for that is the job of Maya. It is the joyous task that has been given to me by Brahman, and I perform it flawlessly. Why do you hesitate? I promise no electric shock is going to make you unconscious.' Maya laughed a little, and her laugh reminded me of temple bells in the distant mountains and of bird song early in the morning. I got up from the rug and moved towards her my heart throbbing rapidly.... My desire to see and feel the woman who called herself Maya had got the better of my discretion. As I walked towards her she got up and I saw that she was of medium height, and held her arms outstretched. It took me an eon to reach her. It was as if everything had been reduced to an extreme slow motion. Finally when I did reach her and touched her hands it was as if a dagger had been thrust into my abdomen. I groaned in pain and fell down in a heap at her feet. I lost consciousness and when I come to, I saw she was near my head tying a poultice on my jaw that had hit the temple ground when I fell.

'Well do you think I am the priest's daughter masquerading as Maya?' she asked gently.

'No, I don't think that .... not any longer.' My jaw was hurting and throbbing.

'You aren't hurt too badly, but I had to give you little gift from myself .... something that would remind you always that Maya is a Supreme power in the cosmos. The thin scar that will remain after the would heals will always remind you of our meeting here in the temple.... a meeting that would otherwise be easily explained away as a hallucination.... do you mind my giving you such a memento?' Maya was smiling again and there was a faint odor of incense emanating from her body. It reminded me of the intoxicating smell of sandalwood.

'I have so much to ask you .... will you meet me again or is this the first and last time that I can share a little bit of your divine time?' I was still in pain and feeling delirious.

'I don't feel upto the task of tackling my fate. I want to retire from the world and live in a hut, without having to compete for petty rewards, when it all comes to nothing anyway! Can you grant me this wish to break away from the mainstream?'

'Gradually you will become stronger spiritually and

mentally. This desire will be placed somewhere in the deep recesses of your deep consciousness. Moreover I had better let you know that before you return to the mainstream you will have already lived for a substantial period in a mountain hut. You will then realize that escaping from reality is not that much fun as is the facing of reality. You must learn to be practical; you must learn to face reality. That is the only choice!' Maya's voice was deeply emotional although in a subtle kind of way.

'There are times when I feel like just sitting down somewhere, and forgetting everyone and everything. I have to fight this feeling, but then sometimes I am not able to see the sense my fated life is supposed to make.'

'Do you think the power that gave you life is interested only in torturing you... that the world that has been made for the enjoyment of man bird, and beast alike is not worth living in?' Maya's voice was deeply concerned.

'One of my plans is to stay for ten years in Sri Turiya's retreat, meditating and living a simple life...' Maya cut in abruptly into my desperate confession.

'Your time with Sri Turiya is strictly limited. he is aware that you want to stay at his retreat, but he is of the old school and likes his privacy as much as you like yours.

'Sooner rather than later you will have little to do with him. You will feel affectionately towards him, no matter where you are. And he will send waves of his love, affection, and goodwill to you through his meditation. After all that is the real issue at stake and not physical proximity!' She sounded annoyed.

'Is there going to be some sort of showdown... some kind of disagreement? That's the last thing that I would want. He has been good to me and taught me a lot.' I was in a state of panic and deep anxiety hit me. It must have been obvious on my face. 'You have only a few more visits left to his place in the next year and then things will fall apart... he cannot tolerate incursions into his privacy. He can never give you shelter for a long period. He has his own agenda. No just that, he feels very irritated by your logical clarity and your questioning his very existence. What do you think, he doesn't have his vanity, pride, ego, and self-delusions.' Maya twirled a red carnation in her hands and looked as if she were talking to a child.

'And what exactly is going to happen to me?' I asked in desperation.

'It is not your fate to be the disciple or student of any master, hidden or otherwise. It is your fate to navigate your life yourself and with the help of very ordinary situations. Remember the ordinary life is the most extraordinary.'

'Do I go back to him or not? Should I just run away?' I was getting totally confused. I had come to the remote hill temple to try and talk to Maya at the instance of Sri Turiya's instructions. The last thing I expected was that Maya would tell me that my association with him was nearing its end.

'You don't have to run away.... at one point he will himself wean you out of his aspiring disciples, and painful though that parting will be it will be in your best interests. The spiritual journey is best performed in the aloneness of your own proximity and it is your fate to do it that way.' Maya gave an amused smile.

'What about my association with you? Is it going to end tonight, or is there some possibility of my being able to contact you at will?' I was anxious to know to what extent my misfortune was establishing itself. My jaw throbbed with pain and I had discovered that one of my molars had also chipped when I fell down after touching

Maya's hands.

'You need not worry about me', she said, 'I'll be there for you always.'

'Thank' God for that', I said with deep relief, 'life without you would be miserable. Either you shouldn't have shown yourself, or you should be available because I have hardly had time to ask you anything. Could I ask you a few questions... the night is getting on, and I can hear the hoot of an occasional owl. Somehow I must try to grasp a few of the ideas behind the Sanatana dharma... can I begin?'

'Go ahead and clear your doubts... You're talking to the right person.' She gave a little laugh and covered her face with her hands. I pushed on doggedly.

'You say that it was you who were entrusted the job of Creation, by Brahman the Ultimate deity., the Eternal Consciousness. What does this really mean?'

'This means that so far as Sanatana Dharma is concerned it was inaugurated by Brahman by taking a part of his undivided consciousness and inaugurating a gargantuan theatre stretching across beyond the stars. That part of consciousness is me. And I am called Maya' which means a mist of luminescence which changes the perspective of the viewer, especially the creatures on earth. It makes them feel that they have enough time to do whatever they want their for own end is far away.. That they have life after life to do what they want.'

'Is Samsara, the doctrine of transmigration true, or is it invented by he priests to control the people through religious and spiritual concepts? Please clarify.

'The doctrine of Samsara is correct, but, the rebirth that takes place may not take place immediately, or on this earth. It could very well take place on another planet in this endless universe.' Maya shrugged as if to say that

I could take it or leave it.

'Are there other planets with life on them.. I mean human life?'

'Naturally ! Some planets are literal replicas of the conditions of this earth, except that they are a much more evolved state , technologically and spiritually. On the other hand the conditions may be much more primitive...'

'Do you mean to say that the very chemical composition and atmosphere of these replicas are such that human life is existing elsewhere in the Universe?.' I found it somewhat threatening hearing these words. To me the comfort of being in a unique planet meant a lot. It made me feel special.

'Don't worry! The humans living on other similar planets do not have predatory designs if their technology is advanced enough. Their intentions are the spiritual uses of technology, and how to apply these for the betterment of their own planet. They have their hands full with their own agenda and this does not include colonizing other similar planets. No volunteers can be found who want to do social work on earth, as their sense of spirituality and practicality tells them that they would be regarded as aliens ... strangers from some other planet.'

'Are they aware of our existence then ? I asked in consternation.

'Yes, many planets with intelligent life know of earth. However this is like the awareness we have of the stars in the night sky. It is a knowledge that does not imply any programmatic agenda. In fact aliens on other planets, who are their form of intelligentsia feel deeply for the plight of the earth, but almost all agree that there should be no interference with the efforts being made here on earth for lasting peace through the spiritual uses of technology.

'What kind of intelligent life exists on these 'advanced' planets .... can an ordinary person make contact with any such civilization?' Her words had aroused my curiosity.

'It is possible, if you get into the subtle body, and get out of the constraints of the gross physical body. Normally such visits to other planets or civilizations are made when the person is sleeping, and the subtle body is released. The body then has properties like those of light and can move even faster—at the speed of thought. The problem is that memories of such journeys are very fuzzy and partial, though the experience is not. The tendency is to write off such memories of other worlds as absurd and inconsequential.

'In fact they are significant in that the best advice often comes from people that a person meets and talks with in a 'bodiless state'. Aha Maya looked silently at me.

'Is it possible to remember these journeys? I seem to be having them almost every time that I sleep at night. My experiences are very coherent and sequential and it appears to me that I benefit greatly from them .... but despite the fact that I feel that a higher inner self is interacting.

'I get only fragments of memory, as to what exactly transpires, in these journeys.' I stopped talking feeling a little exhausted from trying to sound coherent about what is essentially a personal area of exploration. Yet I wanted her input on this are a very urgently.

'Is it possible to remember these journeys ? I seem to be having them almost every time that I sleep at night. My experiences are very coherent and sequential and it appears to me that I benefit greatly from them .... but despite the fact that I feel that a higher inner self is interacting I get only fragments of memory, as to what exactly transpires, in these journeys.' I stopped talking feeling a little exhausted from trying to sound coherent about what is essentially a personal area of exploration. Yet I wanted her input on this very urgently.

' You are asking why memories of the subtle body interacting in alien surroundings are so very vague and contorted .... this is so for very many reasons ...... one of the most valid of these is that if men had solid and vivid memories of other worlds, and all their dreams, then the first thing that would happen is that men would not be able to understand whether they are in the world of the gross or subtle body, and this would create absolute distraction. People who try to remember their experiences in other civilizations during sleep in which the subtle body travels, often run the risk of becoming neurotic, obsessed and even catatonic. Such memories far from being blissful or liberating can trap the intellect in a vicious circle from which it finds very hard to emerge successfully and therefore nature provides a one way valve ....

'I remember one particular journey which has been repeating from my childhood at regular intervals, and causing me anguish and even a feeling of suffocation of sorts... in that journey I feel that I am being suffocated by soft pillows and I am gasping for breath.... this suffocation gives way to a huge desert in which there are deep furrows of sand which cause an unbearable sense of being trapped and confused... finally the furrows move away and there is an incredibly clear plane of perfectly grey desert sand and a feeling of total liberation, of being able to breathe truly and to take life as it comes.... I am not clear about what all this is about, and why it should repeat itself in this way... could you shed some light on this please?' I had voiced a basic concern of mine and wanted to know that the deity who was in front of me in the temple would say about this plight of mine.

'It is fairly clear that the world into which you go in this journey in your subtle body is conveying something of crucial importance to you... basically it concerns life patterns. So far as your life is concerned there will be a cut off point after which you will reach a point of resolution, beyond which you do not suffocate or worry with your inner self. A point will come when you will know factually and inwardly that a man should never alienate the inner spirit as that is the basic and the original sin. It will happen to you years from now but there will be no mistaking it. At that point there will be no major conflicts within your mind. You will not be trapped in petty manoeuvers to become famous or try to gain monetarily. Your sole concern will be service to humanity and this will give you incalculable peace. Yes you will become worthy of me in retrospect, and will reflect on our meeting as a turning point in your life, something that changed the very fabric of your mind and the inclinations of your intellect and senses.' Maya looked at me with concern, and I could sense within her a great compassion that was controlled from flooding out by a sense of will that was like a laser in its intensity. I felt a sense of human love for this young woman who was talking such a high philosophy, and felt dizzy. I had thought Maya might change her form to suit my particular case and therefore give me some respite. I had thought she would come in a body that was old but well preserved. In fact she had come as a frail young beautiful girl almost half my age and telling me ancient wisdom that was not available to me anywhere else. What amazed me the most was that I was talking to her in a manner that I would to any extraordinary young woman and did not feel that I was addressing some kind of apparition or hallucination. It was all too obvious to me that she was the real one and it was I who was the apparition. She was the immortal one and I was only too mortal. Several questions crossed my mind at the point when I realized this but I was careful not to ask trivial questions no matter how appealing they were at that point. However I could not resist myself from asking her what was topmost in my mind.

'Will I ever measure up to the standards of Sanatana Dharma and will I ever become one of the people who contributed something to this ever onflowing river of knowledge... will it be possible for me to be in bliss no matter what are my outward circumstances. As things go now I find it difficult to control the flow of my mind and always have to make compromises on key issues. There are other areas where I find that I do not compromise, but when I don't I often repent my actions and feel that I might be wrong.... in short there is a sort of confusion.' I stopped and smiled a little sheepishly at Maya who looked fresh as the dew on a desert rose. ' I think I must be mad to be talking all this high spirituality with you who are so beautiful that your form would make the best of men breathless... I should be talking all sorts of flirtatious words with you and having the time of my life.... something that I could narrate to my friends even as an adventure I had in the deep forest,... is it not something abnormal to talk so seriously to such an exquisitely beautiful young lady .... is it not a crime not to fall at your feet or to offer you my life.... or even to propose marriage ... I am ashamed at my lack of chivalry and inability to express my concern for this privilege of being in the same space with you in the holy precincts of this mountain temple. Instead I am acting as if you are my Mother and addressing you as if you are twice my age, when you look half of it. Please forgive me I am just a beginner, starting out on the path, and I must be despicable in your eyes....' I was very despondent. and put my head in my hands as it was throbbing with pain. Maya came towards me with light steps and put her right hand on my head. A subtle current of bliss exploded in my brain and spread in swift waves down to my toenails. Although I had not slept at all that night and had taken a journey before that I felt wide awake and fully alert.

'Thank you', I said, 'I feel okay now... I suppose being in your lovely presence would be a bit overwhelming for anyone... even though you are standing beside me I still find it hard to get rid of my disbelief. It seems to me that I am dreaming very vividly, or else have given up the body without knowing how exactly it has happened.' I tried to sound cavalier but couldn't quite make my tone of voice free of concern.

'You have seen something which has taken many lifetimes of consistent efforts and meditation. You should not try to wish it away. Moreover your anxiety that once I disappear, I will go from your life forever is also unfounded .... to the contrary my blessing on you has been that you will see facets of beauty in every woman you see. I am in every woman and a bit of me is in every man. You should not think that Maya has given you nothing. I have given you the blessing of being able to perceive the beauty of the world. The beauty of women and men of all ages, of all colours and climes. Your world will from now on be over brimming with the constant feeling that you are perceiving me in some way. You will see me in a smile, a gesture, a form, ... in anything that catches your eye. You will perceive the music of the earth wherever you go, in bird song, in the laugh of a child, in thunder and in the sweet breezes that flow past the fragrant flowers.... you will see through the rose tinted eyes of love and this will give you uninterrupted bliss... It may take a few hours to settle down but it should be obvious to you that your life has changed from today, that you are no longer the prisoner of your ego.... you have been set free, and set free without any terms and conditions. So tell me what would you like to do for me ? What would you like to do to help humanity ?' Bird song could be heard through the closed door and the rain had stopped. I had no difficulty in understanding what she asked of me.

'Well I would like to write about my experiences with holy sages and above all I would like to write about my meeting with you in this temple.... I can't do this now, because those who read it will find it incredible... .but this memory is not going to fade, instead I will meet you in my mind as often as I need to....' I trailed off somewhat bewildered at what I was saying.

'Write about it... .write whatever you like about it, but don't talk or discuss about it with anyone except Sri Turiya, since he sent you here. You can discuss with him, and even write about what he says but refuse to share this relationship of ours with anyone except on paper! Maya looked like a warrior queen and her eyes flashed fire.

'I agree with this but would you outline your condition', I asked her.

'The problem is not with having a lid on these facts, but that they cannot be digested in seconds. So what is going to happen if you start claiming you had darshan of Maya is that people will find it hard to believe, and you will face embarrassing moments and queries from people whose only interest is to peep into others spiritual life. Even those closest to you will have their doubts, and as a matter of fact, when you do write about it be sure that many people will not understand the significance of what you are communicating.... but there will be a significant section of people who read and hear about your spiritual journey who will be right behind you like a rock.... and frankly it is for these people that you break your silence... by that time it would be only too obvious that you are a mature man, with householders responsibilities, and your confessions will inspire people to reach out to the giddy heights of love and bliss and change thousands of lives all around the world... yes these people for whom you will write will understand the precise nature of your writings, even if they constitute a silent minority'. Maya looked at me with a smile. She was every bit a woman of flesh and blood. Even in the slowly flooding sunlight in the mountains and valleys she was beautiful beyond belief... but something had happened to me. When I looked out towards the sunladen mountain tops it was simply breathtaking. The bird song lifted my spirit making it soar inwards into spiritual silence. Even the frescoes on the temple wall seemed to leap out at me and touch me with their intricate carvings.

'Yes Maya', I said, 'My meeting with you has certainly changed me. For me mountains and birds and the sunlight were things taken for granted.. but now my eyes really seem to have opened and my ears are no longer deaf. Yes, O most powerful of deities you have transformed me in a single night of your presence into a man who is alive and full of the incense of love... I am willing to do anything for you, you just have to let me know, now or at any other time. You have made the pain of life worth it by balancing it with love and beauty. I am indebted to you forever, and your devotee and follower.' I saw a twinkle in her psychedelic eyes.

'No one worships me, they see only the gods and their consorts... very few people in the history of civilization have dared to love the very source of Creation, the deity who created every other deity... so my dear remain in love... And remain in love with me, and you will find me in every turn of the road. I will light up your path with bliss and joy and inwardly you will be full of light, and as the years go by this will be more and more obvious to anyone and everyone... You have been with me for hours on end and I am dressed up in the form of a young full blooded woman, but your mind did not wander towards lust, rather you found your love so intoxicating that at times you were incoherent... as a matter of fact you will find me in all ages and in all forms everywhere around you will be my womb so that you can live in peace and be an oasis of harmony... this is my blessing to you my friend, my lover, my devotee....'

'I constantly get the feeling that you are holding something out on me.... that you want to tell me something but are waiting for me to ask... please don't hold it back, please do let me know... I think I can take it, whatever it is.' I was burning with curiosity.

'There is only one thing to remember and it is pretty simple... your perception of the world of the world has changed, and will continue to explore infinite possibilities... however don't expect too much from the people you meet or those around you... it's not fair to do so. This is a slippery truth but it is the Truth which will guard you and guide you... knowing you inside out I realize that you are prone to expect a bit too much from your friends spiritually speaking. I repeat this is not the right thing to do, because my dear friend it is none of your business to expect spiritual performances from others, no matter who they are. You should just have fun with your friends and forget about teaching them anything, except through your writings or casual comments. Won't this make your life much easier than blowing your breath like a bellows and trying to explain things to them. So if you have to teach anything to your friends it should be to be happy and to laugh... and they will bless you for it. I have handpicked your friends and relatives so that there is mutual delight... so keep this in mind., Maya peered at my chin in concern.

'Yes,' she said , 'It has healed.'

I had forgotten about the fall I had taken deep at night and the poultice she had put there. My hand flew to my chin and I encountered no blood there or raw wound. Instead there was a fine ridge of about an inch which hurt slightly if I pressed it too hard.

'People don't like to meet me because the sign of my cult is a cut on the chin... and this cut is given by me and healed by me so that the power to connect to my intelligence is generated. That is why so few come near me .. .but times are changing and so am I! I no longer need to put this little line on my followers.. they can put in any other diacritical sign... but you insisted that our first full blooded meeting should have a memento. When someone looks at you, they will always realize that you have scaled giddy heights of consciousness and that little line reminds them of this incontrovertible fact.. .you on the contrary seem to have forgotten about it already.'

'You have come as a young and beautiful woman in lovely attire. Is it possible to embrace you like one embraces one's sister or daughter ? I feel a burning desire to touch you.'

'Come then', she said, and stretched out her hands.

I moved forward and embraced her lightly and put my chin on her head. The faint smell of incense came from her sparkling hair and her body was warm. She was no ghost or spirit, she was every bit a woman. We broke apart lightly.

' What makes you think that I can't be a woman of flesh and blood ? I will manifest myself many times to you in different forms, and you will have no desire to know whether you are hallucinating or seeing things in what is called the real world. I will come to you and look after you... you have risked your life time and again for me, in lifetimes past, and in this one.... do you think I am so cold that I will not respond with love... me whose very core is love ?' Maya's eyes flashed like a fire.

I felt a hot flush go down my back and my throat constricted and felt parched.

'Perhaps you were meant for a different Age... and that is why you remained in the oral tradition even when the ancient texts were written down onto scripts... it is very rare to find a woman in the modern world who speaks out her mind and who is not prone to bargaining, be it love or anything else. In any case your presence and words have opened up new vistas for me and it will be many many years before I can talk about you, if not to you'. I felt an anxiety building up in me as the sun rose further on the opposite mountains. Maya was relaxed, completely at ease.

'I will be with you in some form or the other and keep you thinking .... it is only when you come full circle that you will feel that writing about your encounters with me is something that is very natural and normal .... yes at that point in time you will feel that people must know about this.. .the fact that the powers of divinity literally appear in front of their devotees and mingle with the crowds at holy gatherings, making them spiritualized and energized with purity. With you I will come in different forms and with different lessons, and of course you will learn what you already know... only Brahman exists and the rest of us, men animals and deities are but expressions of that Ultimate Power, which exists as a flow of complete bliss but has inaugurated a divine play so that He may enjoy His own power all the more. Really this is the only lesson and once this flows in your veins you will feel quite at ease writing or even talking about it to the relevant seekers. and energized with purity. With you I will come in different forms and with different lessons, and of course you will learn what you already know.. only Brahman exists and the rest of us , men animals and deities are but expressions of that Ultimate Power, which exists as a flow of complete bliss but has in aggregated divine play so that He may enjoy His own power all the more. Really this is the only lesson and once this flows in your veins you will feel quite at ease writing or even talking about it to the relevant seekers. You have already learnt a basic lesson—the deity is not something or someone who comes in a dream, or lies in the imagination. Deities are solid and physical when they want to be, for their devotees, and then they vanish as if a shadow has lifted off the ground.' I looked at her aghast, but still quite in my senses.

'You find that this is a bit strange ? It isn't ! Especially in terrain which is mountainous or stretches out along the rivers of India, especially the Ganga, meditation on a deity is often followed by a deity coming into the life of a devotee. The deity comes as a chance acquaintance or as a friend, or a fellow sadhu who shares knowledge.... this is almost commonplace in this part of the world, and the only problem is that it is the spirit which enters into that person and makes him or her divinely inspired for that duration... it is truly darshan, being in the presence of the Great Divinity who Himself teaches his children and lovers the lessons of love. Yes there are full blown darshans too in which a man or woman of flesh and blood manifests and teaches the devotee lessons in faith and devotion... so please don't be too surprised. Don't think yourself to be unique or the only privileged one... deities appear to their devotees in various ways.... the only difference that I see in you is that you wanted desperately to learn about the Veil of Illusion, about the phenomena of Maya, the most mysterious and hidden of all powers and forces, a power that has beguiled the gods themselves...' Maya tapered off and looked directly at me.

'I don't know why, but most of the time I don't feel as

if you are going to reduce me to ashes or to exterminate me with some extraterrestrial power. Strangely enough I feel quite relaxed and fully at ease with you. I feel with you as I feel in the presence of a good friend... the only thing is that I don't find myself laughing and joking, or taking liberties, and teasing you,' I awaited her reaction.

'In due course of time you will not think of me as a deity, I will have entered your life in a thousand different ways, to the extent your whole life will revolve around me. You will become a mature devotee of mine and take everything in the right spirit of Sanatana dharma which is what it should be.. you will not be just, angry, or indignant with anyone for long and remain established in quietness, blessedness and peace with the friends that the Divine power provides you.... how does it matter whether I am Maya, or a simple village girl catering to your fantasies... what matters is that I love you and you love me and that our interaction should remain within the ambit of our love and not spill over... do you see?' Maya peered into the mountains and sunlight.

'Does the sunshine bother you... that the priest or some villager may see you ?' I was myself somewhat jumpy at this possibility. I would have strange questions to answer.

'Has it not occurred to you that I am Maya, that no one can see me unless I wish it to be so, and no one will remember anything of his interaction with me, including you, unless I permit him to do so... You do not realize that it is now midnight and that we are in a different world now where the sun shines at night and sets during the day...' Maya smiled. I held my head in desperation and there was a cold sweat on my brow. The hands of my clock showed precisely twelve midnight.

'Why don't you let me enter your world permanently and be with you always. I want to go with you now and not leave you for a moment. Let me be your slave forever !' I was serious. That would upset the Divine Plan which is that every man must play his part to the best of his ability before he goes to his beloved deity and enjoys that divine world after a good effort in the world of men' Maya made a mischievous gesture with her hands and I flushed red.

'Which world is this then, it looks somewhat the same to me', I asked genuinely puzzled.

'It is the obverse side of earth', said Maya in a conspiratorial tone of voice.

'What is that supposed to mean ?' I asked her in confusion.

'It is the earth without any of the misery and pain, it is heaven. In this world there is no confusion, no misery, no sorrow, no old age and no death. Those who have successfully completed their tenure on the earth as you know it, come to this heaven where they live indefinitely in their subtle bodies and ruminate on further action in the world. It is a waiting or stopping station between two steps of samsara. Here the rules are different from that on earth as you know it. There are no restrictions of any sort and people here do what they like and are quite unconcerned with what the other is doing'. The false sunrise was receding. By this time I had entirely shifted in to Maya's frame of reference and had resigned myself to whatever it was that might happen. It was not as if I was bewildered or resentful, but that I knew without a doubt that whatever it was that I was experiencing was my responsibility. It was a consequence of my quest for Truth and realization. It was not possible for me to blame anyone except myself.

'Is this place where I will now stay ?' I asked her in consternation.

'No this is just to give you a glimpse of another world

very similar to earth in topography but entirely different so far as the social and cultural side is concerned. In fact at this very moment there are scholars concerning themselves with studies of behaviour in this world. This world too is a station where souls are located before their onward journey to further worlds, but the fact is that no matter what they think when they are on earth, men do not covet strange worlds. This world is almost a mirror reflection of earth and is most sought after. The souls of people come into this orbit if they have been excellent in their field of endeavour, and remain here literally as long as they want without a wrinkle appearing on their faces... despite being here from antiquity it is a young world, and no one ages here. In this world one can choose one's age and one's accomplishments go on getting accumulated. Contrary to expectations there is no moral laxity here and men and women form lasting relationships, going into hundreds of earth years. I have shown you a glimpse of this mirror reflection world to indicate that their is no end of life or awareness after a certain stage of spiritual development. We call this world swarga or heaven because it has everything that we wish it to have. Things materialize in this world by meditating on them, or simply cogitating on them. There is no money or currency and no property. All these can be conjured up simply by focussing on what is required. There is no need for food or drink but they can be had by the subtle body in terms of taste alone but not physical ingestion... look eat this apple !' Maya held out a red apple to me. I took it and began to eat it. It was a peculiar sensation since I could feel the succulence of the fruit and its juice but it never traveled down to my stomach and remained till my throat alone.

'The subtle body does not require any physical food but regenerated itself through meditation cogitation...however any kind of food is available in this world simply by wishing for it... it is treated as a kind of diversion, because the subtle body neither really eats or digests any kind of food. There are no wastes as the subtle body is cleansed in the sunshine of the Lord's love, and refurbished with energy by cogitating on the love of the Lord.' Maya explained

'You mean this world is everyman's dream come true ?' I asked 'Approximately', she laughed.

'Frankly speaking I feel rather uncomfortable here' I said uneasily. All the people that I saw going on their business seemed to be deeply preoccupied with something. They didn't seem to be much interested in anyone else. I also saw that there were a few people sitting in the shelter of a tree and gazing into the distance. In fact gazing thus seemed to be the most popular form of meditation. It seemed to be a perfect world where the body of the denizens was between twenty and thirty years and no one was too thin or too fat. Everyone seemed healthy and dressed well. To my right on a mountain I could see a very swanky architectural wonder.

' What is that ?' I asked Maya.

'That is where anyone who wants can go and eat or sleep or meditate absolutely free of charge.' She said.

'It must be flooded with people', I observed.

'Not exactly,' said Maya. That building is a sort of creche for new arrivals in this worlds where those who have just died on earth and have meritorious karma can come and adjust gradually to the new perfect way of living . It is there that they can locate their friends and ancestors in this world and make contact with them. Yes, the building is very airy and lighted up, and this makes the stay of the people there a very comfortable one, but sooner or later everyone leaves for the happy hunting grounds of the wider world'.

'There don't seem to be any motor cars, airplanes, buses and so on' I observed.

'Here everything operates on the power of thought. You can go wherever you want, or contact anyone you want just by thinking about it in a focused manner. This in itself is a technique which has to be mastered, but most people here don't seem to have much difficulty with it' she said.

'It seems to me that it would be appropriate to call this the realm of the intellectual world, or the world of the mind, or of consciousness... there is certainly a sense of freedom from gravity although some glue like force does exist and keeps one from just flying off as if one were in space' I hesitated thinking I may have spoken too much.

'You're right this is the chidakash, or the realm of mind consciousness where it is possible to project one's thought in any way and any direction possible. You can create almost anything or meet almost anyone... it is a real but mostly suited for living a spiritual and creative life. Who would you like to meet, anyone in particular?'

'No', I said 'You are more than enough for me and I don't want to do interviews of famous men. They suddenly don't seem all that relevant anymore !'

'Being rich or famous isn't that important', she said.

'Then why is it that most people think of nothing else except fantasies about what they would do if they came into a lot of cash or if they were very famous ?' I wanted to know her position on the craze for being rich and famous.

'It is like an incurable itching to be rich and famous for then the individuals feel that they can satisfy their every whim and fancy so far as pleasures and enjoyment is concerned. It is a fact that the moment that pleasure have to be satisfied there comes into play a desire to have loads of money that can buy whatever it is, whether it is sensuality or gluttony.' She smiled and looked over the hills where time seemed to have stood still and a triple rainbow was stretched out over the valley in the mountains.

'Do you want money and fame ?' Maya asked me point blank.

'Well there must be something you could do with that... I mean there are men and women who use their money and fame to do good in the world, help people and be good themselves... I think if ever I came into a lot of money and became very famous I could do things for society, for self knowledge !' I was a bit wary as to what her response might be now that I had taken my stand.

'You're missing the point... the real power that a person has is his imagination and time... the work in society and for society should be respected fully and participated in, but to spend all one's time in trying to uplift society does not seem a very good option for you because all these organizations for upliftment of society are sooner or later involved in social work and try to make people aware of themselves. So long as the initial inspiration is there the organization for spiritual upliftment goes forward and attracts a lot of people, but as soon as this initial inspiration dies, and some tomb or samadhi is made for such a person then the entire system becomes mechanical and the people who control the organization themselves resemble a corporate structure. The prayers, meditations, daily routines and annual events resemble those of any organization. So what I am saying to you is that if you ever become rich or famous even to the extent that you may visualize it would be much better to see the world, help the needy people by building institutions of education and religiosity without doing too much time expenditure on them, and with the full realization that by the time they will be reaching their flowering you will be an old man and have hardly anything to say about them, and then your name will live on.... is that your ambition ?!' Maya doubled up with laughter and mirth while I squirmed uncomfortably.

'I am sorry but I am all too human, but I do see what you mean, because I think the other plan I have is to travel around the country and the world, to see it's beauty and to enjoy and sense of release that comes with movement'. I still felt that I had something to say about the rich and the famous.

'Travel is very fine but at the end of the day it is a person's spiritual concentration that counts. However certain bits of movement in the globe are written into a persons life and no one really remains static in one place. Swarga is the place to travel, just focus on a place in this or any other world you can catalogue and off you go like a mist... no visas and tickets ! The people who live in swarga are the ones who are the really rich in karma and they can spend these karma at very good value until the end of their endlessly long lives !' Maya looked at me with twinkling eyes, which lit up with the fire of intelligence.

'I want to travel with you in this world at least to one or two places. Would you agree and how is one to do that ?, I asked after I had calmed down.

'Do you want to go in this world or some other world ? Let me ask you what type of world you would like to go to? Would it be one of the plains, or that of the mountains. Do you want to go sailing over lakes or be part of life in some metropolitan ? Think about it a bit and let me know ! I will take you with me and be with you and once you have traveled in the mind you will never have the bug to travel in machines and go through all those constricting procedures. That's not travel, that's torture !'

'I would be only too grateful if I could fly with you', I said half seriously to her, and I would like to do a brief whirlwind tour with you of some of the more interesting places in Swarga'.

'Then you would have to visit a few of the places that are of natural beauty. I would have suggested that you meet some of the deities, but that you can do as and when you like much later. For unlike myself who is a little known entity in the Hindu pantheon and has perhaps very few temples if any consecrated to her, the gods are very popular, and there are millions of them... let us do our profound namashkar to them but let us not reveal what they say or do to us. So even if we go their ashrams or temples we cannot do much except to give their blessings to humanity, that is their brief benedictions to their devotees'.

'In fact I have a burning desire to meet Lord Ganesh and the other deities of the pantheon... I am sure they would have a beneficial impact on my life.' I was burning with religious fervour and sincerely believed in what I was saying.

'You can have these journeys in your gazing meditations and that would be much better than a guided tour of Swarga. In fact right now I have plucked your gazing attention and directed it into a different channel. What you are interested in is discussing with Sri Turiya certain aspects of the spirituality of Sanatana Dharma. Let us keep in mind that it is he who has sent you to the temple in which your body is sitting cross legged right now even as your consciousness flies with me. But yes we can have a look at Lord Ganesh. Look at that river in the distance and focus... right now here we are! What do you see?' Maya chuckled gleefully. I was stunned. In front of me was a large man with the face of a elephant. He was sitting on the river bank of a stream that was sparkling as if it were alive. The deity was sloshing water over himself and making sounds and exclamations of satisfaction. It was Lord Ganesh, and he emanated such friendly vibrations that it was impossible to be tense in his presence. But I had begun having a problem in concentration and the air around seemed to come in waves rendering everything I saw fuzzy. I felt myself falling off a precipice and after an inordinately long and frightening duration I landed with a thud on solid ground. I felt myself anxiously to see if anything was broken or smashed but I was alright. I was sitting against the temple wall where I had started gazing the previous night and the dawn had crept out over the hills. The events of the night were etched clearly in my mind, and it was clear that I had successfully gazed into another dimension. However my sense of panic was more than my sense of excitement. What was remarkable was the fact that I could recall even small bits of conversation or discussion that I had with the deity Maya and was not in the least confused about my experience. However at that point I wanted to get away from the temple as fast as possible and reach back to Sri Turiya's retreat. I went to the temple spring and drank my fill of cold water and splashed my face with it, and made my way down the path to the bus stop. Hardly a soul stirred as I made my way carefully down the path to the road head some kilometres down hill and I went downhill as fast as the path would permit.

At the road head the tea stall was already selling glasses of tea and I had one. After what seemed an inordinately long delay one bus came, and it was almost empty. I jumped inside and took a seat with a view towards the valley. The sunrise and bird song was incredible and I felt I had returned home. Never had I felt more at home in the mountains and appreciated them in this way. At the same time a strange drowsiness overcame me and I slipped off to a deep sleep awakening only when my bus stop was approaching. I rubbed the sleep from my eyes and went up the hill path at a steady pace my heart pounding. It was as if I was still in the other world into which I had gazed last night. It didn't seem like the last night, rather it seemed almost a season earlier. Yet the memory of it was so clear that I was at a loss to explain as to what exactly had happened. According to my categories, I had had an extraordinarily successful gazing session and had met my favorite deity Maha Maya the perpetrator of the Universe, the force that make life worthwhile for most people, the flimsy curtain that had to be parted before one entered into Moksa of Brahman. Indeed I was still reeling over the sheer beauty of the goddess and the melody of her voice, the precision of her diction and the sharpness of her logic, when Sri Turiya's retreat came into view around a bend in the hill.

I wondered as I walked those long last few steps towards Sri Turiya's retreat how much I should tell him of what I had experienced. Indeed I wondered how much of my experience he would be able to take for real and not write off as some kind of hallucination. I felt if I told him an unexpurgated version of what I had experienced he would write me off as deranged and ask me to go home never to return. Maya herself had warned me that I should be very careful with him and that I had only a few visits to his place left in my destiny. As such I did not want to jeopardize my chances of have a few discussions, conversations, and debates with Sri Turiya as he was a man with a great deal to offer the inquisitive mind so far as the spiritual life was concerned. As I walked down those last few steps towards his balcony which was empty at that point in time as the sun was now out in full force I decided to play it like a true disciple of my Isht Devi, Maha Maya and to tell him only that much which would not make him feel that I had

had an experience that could easily be classified as out of the ordinary. I decided as I rang the temple bell hanging near the ground floor that I would play it very close to the chest and not tell him of my conversation with Maya. This was not because I distrusted Sri Turiya, but because I felt at that time that the conversations I had with Maya were not to be discussed with anyone else at that point in time. In fact it felt as if I would be betraying a trust of some one I loved with all my heart and soul. I felt strongly then that the conversation I had had with Maya was less a dialogue between deity and devotee, than lover and beloved. At the same time I was quite aware that this reticence on my part was also going in the long run to create a barrier between me and Sri Turiya and I was already sure that this was perhaps my last visit but one so far as Sri Turiya's retreat was concerned. I had found my love and although I respected Sri Turiya I had realized after meeting Maya that I did not love him in that passionate way . He now seemed too self centred and dry after what I had been through with Maya. I did not have an iota of doubt that I could contact the goddess through gazing and could focus on her through meditation. I was aware that Sri Turiya, who demanded absolute obedience in a patriarchal sense would sense that something was amiss, but I was equally sure I could drag on our conversations at least another week after this visit. My concern was to visit him once again in October and clear some of my doubts. It was not as if I could not have contacted Maya for these doubts but I was not interested in too many dry academic debates with her. On the other hand Sri Turiya specialized in hair splitting and joking and making fun and was the perfect yogi so far as spiritual knowledge was concerned. He and I would have had a much longer association if he had been willing to allow me some of my youthful impetuosity's rather than being determined to discipline me and make me behave like a middle-aged monk which I found very hard to do.

Further my relations with Ma Turiya had always been a bit strained as I was not able to let go with her, though I did not feel constrained in her presence. Her being a white also made me feel that she did not really understand what was going on in the Sanatana Dharma. I admit on hindsight that this was a most heinous ethnic type of judgement but I must confess that I did suffer from it. Further another devotee and his wife had already started booking their berth as the caretakers of Sri Turiya and Ma Turiya. They were to have an adjacent room and to take care of all the needs of the holy couple doing 'service' to their 'guru'.

My problem was that I was having a crisis of faith, and after my meeting with Maya this had stepped up to gargantuan proportions. I knew I could not compete with that couple both of whom were worldly wise and very practical. In those days I was very naive and did not know how to impress others or please them. Rather I became wooden and stiff whenever I had to 'please', others and this I knew was going to be my undoing in Sri Turiya's place. The only people who understood me were my parents who knew that I was an honest fellow who found it hard to be hypocritical.

Suddenly Sri Turiya was there in front of me on the balcony in all his majesty and my fears fell to the ground. I knew that he was fond of me and I loved and respected him to the best of my capacity.

'How are you, my friend', he greeted me from the balcony.

'Alright, I guess', I replied in a shy tone.

'Ma, get us some coffee, he's looking in need of it', said Sri Turiya in an affectionately imperial tone that he used sometimes when he talked to Ma.

'Hello, little fellow', said Ma, 'what have you been

upto. You look all tired and sleepy'. She was concerned about me.

'I spent a lot of time meditating inside the temple' I said, 'and although my mind is refreshed I think my body is a bit tired. I should be okay after some coffee', I said briefly.

'I'll give you some doughnuts as well' said Ma affectionately. And now that Ma is no more I feel that she put all her love and affection into those glasses of coffee, those doughnuts and flour cakes. She was really a wonderful person to have known, completely unassuming and devoted to the Master, who rode her like a reversal of the goddess Durga and her tiger.

The coffee and doughnuts came and Sri Turiya opened the gambit in a casual way.

'How was your meditation, little fellow', said Sri Turiya in a most concerned and affectionate tone, 'Do let me know about it, and what did you see in your gazing.... anything to report and tell us.. tell us some of it. It's off the tourist map but it's a well known temple to the sadhus and yogi's who live around this area and to go and meditate there has almost always changed the direction of the Yogi or aspirant who went there . They almost always saw or dreamt or felt something in that temple. That is why the local people have kept themselves from proclaiming too loudly about it's virtues'. Sri Turiya stopped and looked at me with a grin.

'Good coffee!' he said with a grin and then laughed loudly.

'Come on relax, drink your coffee and have a doughnut', he said and went on to have a long sip himself.

I was in a quandary. My experience had centred around Maya and she was the last deity that I wanted to mention, but that was what I had gone there for in the first place itself. I decided to speak out in measured tones and in generalities without getting too specific, especially about the fact that I found the physical beauty of the goddess overpowering beyond belief.

'I don't know how to put it, but I had an extraordinary night at the temple and I still don't know how to explain what happened there. There is nothing I want to hide but don't know how to go about telling you and Ma about it....' I trailed off in confusion.

'There's nothing to be confused about, my dear, it's obvious to me that you have found your path and goal. This is an unusual path and I want to confirm that Maya has accepted you as a disciple. In which case we can wind up our conversations the next time you come and you can go on your way with her and she will manifest as man, woman and child to take you across your journey in life... she is a prime deity although not normally worshipped and indeed feared by those travelling on the spiritual path... strangely you seem to have an affinity towards her and you show no signs of fear at all. In fact your face indicates that you are deeply infatuated by her, and this is the price she demands from her devotees... that they worship the dust on which she treads'. Sri Turiya got up and started pacing the balcony with a frown on his face.

'Is it something to do with me ?', I asked reverentially.

'I want you to do one thing which is the ultimate test for me that Maya has accepted you. If as he has accepted you my role in your life from now on will be to round off our friendship and stop thinking about you since you will be in capable hands..., indeed more capable than mine.,' Sri Turiya was sounding a bit hesitant.

'Please tell me what I should do ? Kindly do not hesitate !' I pleaded.

'My dear friend I want you to close your eyes and think of any fruit in your mind. Once you have formed a mental picture of it you are to stretch out your right hand and clasp this fruit. I want to see what happens, if it is okay with you... understand this is only a request, and please don't divert this conversation before we go through this, okay ?' Sri Turiya looked at me with a most penetrating look, something that I can recall now even after twenty years. His dark brown eyes were brimming with concern and love and pierced me with his affection.

'Alright', I said , 'I will do it from your seat in the balcony'.

'Done', said Sri Turiya. I shifted to Sri Turiya's poof and quieted my mind down till it was still and then thought of an apple. I visualized it as being of medium size and a shiny red in colour. Once this image had stabilized I reached out and caught it with my hand my eyes still closed. I felt something solid in my right hand and opened my eyes with a shock. In my right fist was a shiny red apple ! I was stunned and shocked, because I felt that to some extent I was humoring Sri Turiya and that the end result of the experiment would be a zero.

'There seems to be an apple in your hands, my friend, and it's an apple which is out of season as the apples haven't started coming yet'. Sri Turiya's voice was pensive and grave as if he were reflecting on the impending death of a dear and near relative.

'What's this supposed to mean, Sir ?' I asked in consternation.

'This has less to do with me, and more with Maha Maya' said Sri Turiya with a wagging of this little finger.

'What exactly do you mean ?' I asked handing him over the succulent shining apple.

'Well, when Maya accepts a disciple she makes him

a characteristic gift, a gift that makes the disciple carefree... he can materialize anything, anytime, anywhere... and that seems to have happened in your case, and if you want to try it out again we can go in for it one more time.' Sri Turiya was serious all the way through. This was certainly not the sage I knew who would laugh at every thing and make jokes about the most sacred aspects of his devotees lives. Sri Turiya was dead serious.

'Alright', I said with determination, 'Let's do it again'.

'Think this time of a diamond ring which is encrusted in gold. It should be big enough to fit on the little finger of your right hand. Okay ?' Sri Turiya's concern was evident in his voice. There was also a subdued excitement which was contagious. It took me a long time to calm down my mind, before I could properly visualize the diamond ring. Once I had visualized it clearly enough to see it sparkle in my mind consciousness I put out my right hand and clasped it. I felt a light object in my hand and when I opened my eyes there was a diamond ring in my hand. I put it on the little finger on my right hand. It fitted as if it had been custom made for it. The diamond was large as a pea and sparkling in the daylight.

'Here you are', I said to Sri Turiya' take it as a gift from me'. Suddenly the tension broke down and we started finding the situation comical and even hilarious. We roared with laughter and doubled up as we observed each other laughing. Ma had joined in and was equally effusive.

'This whole thing has gone too far' I said in protest 'soon you will be telling me to go into business... first become a fruit vendor, and then a jewel merchant... our problems are over !' Of course I was joking but this remark caused further merriment among us. The few villagers passing by on the path below looked at us as if we had gone out of our minds.

It took a long time for us to settle down before our jibes at each other had reached an end.

'This is really a serious matter', said Sri Turiya' something that deserves a little more attention, of a different sort., He was still wiping his face with a hand towel and his eyes were red. This was the Sri Turiya that I loved and admired. A person who could let go and be a child and experience the joy of eternity without any sense of self consciousness or shame. I knew then as I know now that Sri Turiya, exacting though he was, had a great fund of love and affection for me and indeed for all the people he knew. His special love for me was because of my desperation and obsession to learn spirituality at his feet.

'Firstly', said Sri Turiya, ' what are we going to do with the apple and the ring ? I think we ought to find out what we are supposed to do about these divine gifts.' He appeared to be a bit hesitant. 'You brought them around' said Ma 'What do you think we should do about them ?'

'I think we should eat the apple as prasad and try to return the ring back to Maha Maya.... with a request to take away this gift, which is something that would only be an encumbrance on my path. If I have no challenge to earn my living and have some sort of El Dordado in my mind I don't think it would be possible to have a firm head on my shoulders. I want to experience the life of an ordinary man, so that I can reflect on the life of an ordinary man, write and try to link Sanatana dharma to everyday battles and conflicts...' I felt a little dizzy and I stopped.

'We have heard this from you in many different situations and in many different words, but how is this going to happen? said Ma softly.

This was when Sri Turiya displayed his genius. He raised his right hand to the skies and gave a smile.

'I've got it', he said 'Let's eat the apple, and with prasad will come the spiritual current of the great deities and we shall know what to do with the ring... one thing is for sure, we don't want to be magicians !' Sri Turiya looked enquiring at me and shook his head.

'That's absolutely true' I said enthusiastically. Ma cut the apple and we ate a piece each and gave a piece to the bhakta who came to clean the retreat and put some before the household deities.

I still cannot confirm it but the eating of that apple put me in such an elevated level of consciousness that I could see my life stretched out like a huge textured carpet in front of me. Nothing was hidden. We didn't have to debate anything among ourselves. It was obvious that the ring had come from another world and had to go back there. I sat down and wished that it was leaving and when I opened my right fist in which I had placed it, it was gone. It was also obvious to me that with this act of reversal and non acceptance, the power vested in me to materialize goods had been mandatorily taken away from me. From somewhere within the recesses of my mind and psyche I heard the slow swish of the breeze of eternity which sounds so much like the windblown pine trees. I was absolutely convinced that Maya was luxuriating in the conviction that I loved her for who she was and not for what she could give me in terms of material profits.

The piece of apple so elevated our levels of consciousness that none of us wanted to pass the time in talk and we each retreated to our corners to meditate. Although I had been exhausted when I came to the retreat I was fresh as a dewdrop and I had a beautiful meditation, in which I felt that I was a drop in a crystal clear lake, cool amidst the heat of the midday sun. There were no thoughts and ideas and no visions. It was undifferentiated, unalloyed bliss. When I opened my eyes it was evening, and the sun was touching the distant peaks in a soft yellow light. Sri Turiya and Ma had gone for a walk and there was nobody around the retreat so I sat on the stone bench waiting for them to come back. It was hard to believe that I had spent the last night and day almost without a blink of sleep and was not still feeling the need to sleep. In fact I had a lot to discuss with Sri Turiya, and so far as I was concerned the discussion hadn't even begun. I braced myself for the night ahead with Sri Turiya and Ma. I was excited at last and waiting with anticipation as to what they would say about some aspects of my meeting with Maha Maya in her form as a nubile hauntingly beautiful young woman.

Sri Turiya would not have been the Master that he was had he gone straight into a dry discussion of my experiences with Maya in the hidden temple. Instead he displayed his mastery by ordering a 'celebration'. To his devotees this meant to have some good food and coffee before we retired to one of the rooms in the retreat and began laughing and joking before he finally turned the conversation to 'serious' matters.

Moreover my ambivalent feelings towards the Master seemed to have come in check and I could view him with unalloyed love and affection. It was my tremendous good fortune in this life to have met the Master and to have imbibed his terrific sense of fun and laughter. He had instilled in me an attitude in which he taught me never to get too serious about anything and to take things as they came with a pinch of salt. At first when I was a young man I suffered because of this attitude which was taken as being frivolous. I also suffered because my interest in mundane things was so vague that I took a very long time coming to know of the nitty gritty of things. Gradually with a concerted effort I came to realize that I needed to keep in mind some basic aspects of institutional reality in mind. By the time I was in the thick of life and alone except for the goddess I adored I had to take recourse to her alone. My links with Sri Turiya at that time were all but over and I had hardly any interest in him, as I had imbibed what I could from him and gone my way.

We ate a hearty meal and settled down with a glass of freshly ground coffee in the smaller room feeling replete in the love filled cooking of Ma.

'I don't think we need anything after a meal like that .... except a good sleep', said Sri Turiya laughing uproariously. Ma joined in the laughter and they had a moment of deep communion, in which I shared fully. The fact was that I was over the years more than a devotee or aspirant to Sri Turiya, I was his spiritual heir, his son. This was a berth not reserved just for me but for anyone who had that type of kinship with him and with Ma.

'Let's go about this with your patent objection about me and my way of living.. go ahead and attack me with my claim to happiness, not being in keeping with my sources of livelihood !' Sri Turiya's eyes twinkled.

'You know that there is only one difference between us, and absolutely none other... I dispute your right to live off the donations of others, and yet claim to be their master and teacher. This is something I find hard to understand... please tell me about it just one more time, and I promise neve to bother you again about it. I mean to me it is important to have my own source of income... it is my sign of independence. I realize that I may be making a stupid statement, and being even egoistic to an extraordinary degree. What's worse I may be acting ignorant and just not being able to understand. So do please say something about it'. I fell silent after what was rather an impassioned plea.

The master addressed me by name affectionately and told me that spiritually I was his son and anything that a son asked his father for he should get from his father, if he could give it.

'This is something that is very easy to understand... your ego is coming in the way of grasping that there is nothing wrong in a master begging for his food or that money is put in his begging bowl. I don't have that kind of problem and have never had it. When the money gets too much I give it to those who are needy and there have been times when I have slept hungry nights and days on end. One day you will reach the same position, and you in your own way will not care two hoots for money, or how much of it anyone has or has not. My experience is that one should have enough for one's needs and not enough to become addicted to pleasure. You will realize one day when I am no longer physically in your life that there is no shame in accepting money or any kind of donation from a friend or a devotee. After all why do I accept the love and affection of those who are close to me... following your logic I shouldn't accept it from anyone except perhaps Ma, who loves me to distraction. But no! I accept your love for me and from so many others. As you have already realized this is not really an issue and you just pretend that it is.You are not the Master that you will become in your time... at that point you will have no problems in accepting love even from a beggar or a leper, not just from your beautiful goddess Maya!' Sri Turiya had spoken with passion and there was a silent fury in his words. Yes! I had understood!.

There was a long silence in the room and we could hear the cicadas making their hypnotic chirruping, the sound coming in higher and lower cadences from the world just outside the retreat. I looked at Sri Turiya as he sat to my right. Yes, the man had made peace with his destiny. He truly was a hidden master who would remain hidden until it was too late for anyone to bring him into the mainstream. He had already become a legend in his lifetime, to be referred to with only a handful of people who really knew him. He had paid off his debt to humanity and given a few tasks of love and affection to his close ones. Yes, he had succeeded in his life and remained unsullied and happy even in the face of pain suffering and adversity. He was a lion of a man and his very eyes, beard and face belied the fact.

'Can we talk a bit of my experience with the goddess?' I asked 'I'm completely sure she warned you against me', he said slowly 'Well she said I could discuss with you', I said confidently.

'What else?' he enquired a bit warily.

'She said my visits to you would soon end and that I was now becoming a bit of an irritant to you and impinging on your privacy'. I felt that I had to let him know the truth.

'The fact of the matter is that your path is soon to diverge from mine and you could come again and talk to me. It seems better that if you stay a little longer this time and finish off all pending discussions rather than come again. You have your path and I have mine and the goddess was right in letting you know that you should walk on your own now'. Sri Turiya spoke in a voice that I had almost never heard before. He seemed agitated and nervous, and almost out of control.

'If you feel that we should call it off, and you don't want to discuss, then do let me know about it'. I was myself almost furious for some reason.

'This is all due to lack of sleep, my son, what we have experienced in a small period of time is taking its toll.

We must get some sleep, each one of us, especially you and I promise that I will take you on in any discussion about Maya or life in general the whole of tomorrow, even if it goes again into the deep night. But now we must rest and recuperate' Sri Turiya's voice was tired and I suddenly realized how exhausted I was myself, and in fact amazed at what I had been through. How stupid of me I thought, to be so greedy, even if it was for spiritual knowledge. I readily agreed to his suggestion. I touched his feet and walked wearily down to the ground floor where I had my bed and lay down on it.

As I looked on the roof of the small room swirls of mist came in waves before my eyes and through them a face smiling and blowing benedictions my way. I did not know when I fell asleep into a deep dreamless sleep that was broken only by the bird song at dawn. I lay down and said my mantra and went over what I wanted to discuss with Sri Turiya. A strong sense of power surged through my veins. I was completely myself again, and not in the least nervous or agitated.

After an early morning breakfast we sat in the balcony staring out at the lovely mountains stretching outwards and the gentle hiss of the wind all around us. I had given Sri Turiya a gist of what had transpired at the temple.

'Your gazing obviously took you out of your body and into the realms of Maya. Yet she cut the journey short when you had a darshan of Lord Ganesh. This means she doesn't want you to get involved with the worship of the Gods. She wants you to follow her instructions and to follow her path. Well the great power that she is, most people are frightened out of their wits just at the mention of her name. Here comes along someone who is almost obsessively interested in her... naturally she is pleased. On the other hand our lottery opens and you who want to get on without the help of physical gurus are in for a bonanza. To be accepted by Maya in any measure, however small means that you will not only reach your goal of moksa, but that you will reach it in the most interesting way possible for you. Do you understand? All that I could offer you was the life of a recluse who meditates on reality and has intense discussions with his master... but she has offered you infinitely more... from your eyes I can see she has already hypnotized and mesmerized you. In a sense that is good, because your path is clear and she will herself draw you forward, step by step and take you into her circle of power. My dear friend your journey is over, you just have to take the steps.. .at the same time you have been a good and steady friend of mine, though separated by the years you and I have shared and will continue to share an abiding bond of love and affection.. so I must share with you the outline of my path a path which I adopted when I met my guru, and when he told me to trod it on my own.' Sri Turiya looked towards me, his eyes were glazed with emotion.

'Do tell it to me Sri Turiya, anything you have to say will be of utmost value to me because I sense that we are in the process of saying goodbye, so far as spiritual discussions are concerned'. I was very eager to hear what he had to say and was literally leaning forward in my seat. I could see in the air a large eagle going round in circles and the sight haunted me. That's what I wanted to do myself. To be free and flying high above the cares of the world, untouched in any personal way by sorrow and misery. Yet caring deeply for everyone that I knew.

'When the disciple steps out of the shadow of his teacher the teacher always gives him a gift of knowledge. So far as I am concerned I will tell you the knowledge that I live by, this is the knowledge of the Other, or the 'something else'. In this world that we live there is 'something else', or 'something other', that decides what we do and how we do it is left to us. In short the set and setting is put up by the power that we can only perceive, but which has no specific name or shape. Yes the ancient seers have given it a name, and even today the sadhus and seers provide it with endless names.. there must be millions of them. That is not what I am referring to. Beyond and over these names there is a power that decides everything and gives everyone a chance to perform within a particular theatre, or theatrical context.

'If one is aware that there is an 'other' then there is a gradual honing up of our skills of interaction, no matter how vast or limited our theatre of action. In fact ancient seers always pointed out that the way we reacted and acted within a context decided our fate, not in the next world alone, but in the present one also.

'For example in the story of the Mahabharata there is an endless reference to the 'other' which goes so far as to make even Sri Krishna subject to the 'other' and deeply cognizant of it. Indeed every word or gesture is important as it goes down into the records of the other which are taken into account in the doctrine of samsara which is used or invoked to decide where the consciousness of a person goes after physical cessation.

'So also in the Ramayana there is Ram who is aware of the 'other', and bases his every action on the prodding of the 'other'. Have you ever pondered why Sri Ram did not revolt against his aged father and decide to accede to the throne despite his father's later change of mind due to the will of his step mother Kaikeyi ? The 'other' is an intelligence with which we live and something that communicates to us in myriad ways. But to understand the message or the direction that it is indicating one has to be very aware and alert. If one is not completely alert the signal it gives us will not be apprehended. In fact the gurus of my line sought to keep themselves in a state of being where the 'other' could almost live their lives for them. This is not a question of giving up all claims to an individuality, or of becoming totally passive but of being able to read the flow of events and to interpret one's role in them'. Sri Turiya gestured for me to comment.

'I understand what you mean', I said and I meant it.

'It is not a question of simply understanding it in some intellectual way but of cultivating one's relationship with the world, the environment so that it literally speaks to you in it's own particular language. This is a language which over passage of time becomes so clear that it is almost an iron writ, something that cannot be ignored. Whether one is capable of following the instructions of the other or not is not the issue. There are occasions when a man is no position to follow the prodding's of the other even though he knows he must. He may not follow them because he doesn't have the energy or is afraid of the consequences... but not to follow the prodding's of the 'other' is an act of immorality, because to those whom the 'other' has manifested itself, it is their *Ultimate Companion*. The 'other' is a personalized God with no particular form or content. It is a relationship with the infinite creation and it is miraculous because in the grandiloquent universe it communicates with little men like us and advises us on what to do in face of uncertainty. It teaches us to make our decisions after having provided cues as to what one should do...this is the path I follow, and it is this that tells me more than what you have told me that you will go your own way. That mark on your chin tells me that Maya has adopted you in toto and that she has for some reason accepted you as a responsibility. She has sent you back to me so that I can tell you about the 'other' because in a very real way she is the 'other' for you who will manifest in different ways and shapes, and give you messages of love and hope..' I came in at this point of his discourse. A few questions were burning in my mind.

'What does it mean to establish a relationship with the other?' I asked.

'It is a two way link.. it is a question of the 'other' finding a worthy man who would have the strength to follow its instructions... most of the time we all know what to do but somehow are unable to follow our insight. So it is important to be the type of person to whom a clue can be of any use in terms of practicality, else the communications which go on and never give up will be useless and soon they will not even be noticed. It is a strange fact of life that the more one listens to the 'other' more it 'talks' to one, and a moment comes when one's whole life is nothing except a sort of symphony which is being played out of sheets of music which have been arranged by the 'other'. Do you understand?' Sri Turiya was looking out into the skies. A few clouds dotted the sky.

'I understand what you mean and perhaps have been following what you say in my own way, but what I wanted to ask you is that how does one nurture contact with the 'other'?'. I was very eager to know.

'As I mentioned it is a question of putting in your claim... of becoming available to the 'other', and then realizing that there is no better way to proceed in life, apart from it being actually the only 'right' way. Usually a person proceeds purely from his thinking centre or from his emotional centre. Both have their limitations because these centres can be very stubborn and get stuck in a wrong interpretation that could literally ruin a man, or take him to the brink..' I came in at this point.

'That's what I mean', I said , 'how does one know that one is making the 'right' interpretation? After all in any art it takes some practice to be able to make manoeuvres, and in the art of spirituality it must be even more difficult. I mean if one doesn't have an aptitude for it what you are saying would only be a fascinating theory, a kind of wonderful hypothesis which could be debated and pruned, but not practiced'.

'Yes, to many people, this can just be a theory, and at best an interesting one, but for me and you it is the very rudder of our lives. My friend there are powers of the spirit which are way beyond your or my intellect, and to hand over decision making to one's power of reasoning could be catastrophic. Even men who are not schooled or have a low degree of literacy are many a time very successful in leading a happy life because they have an inkling of the 'other', accept it's existence, and follow its cues in their lives in an almost instinctive way. On the other hand the super industrialized societies, of which I have some firsthand exposure deify the thinking power in man, and make a sort of eccentric situation occur where decisions go right and wrong in alternating rhythms. Such heavy dependence on the thinking centre creates problems in relationships and these are very strained and under stress the more educated a person is. The higher the level of formal education the greater the stress of living because it is the job of the thinking centre to block the signals coming from the realms of the 'other'. To catch these signs and symptoms and signals there has to be a still mind and it is the job of the thinking power in us to go on thinking in circles, upward and downward spirals. Moreover to accept the 'other' means that one has surrendered one's ego and vanity at the altar of the vast 'other' , which directs our lives, if we wish it to do so and can sacrifice our wild illusions of being supreme in a world where everything is but a passing fantasy!'

'I don't know about the next person' I said, 'but I seem

to grasp what you are saying with little difficulty.. and I think it is entirely due to my exposure to the goddess in the temple. She had made so many little gestures as she spoke that it was like being exposed to a new dimension in language and I had come to understand for the first time in my life that communication is more than just a verbal effort. She tuned me in many ways which are still submerged in me to be able to decipher the environment, including people, in a way that could be said to border on the miraculous. I think I am totally with you and that what you are saying is wholly palatable and acceptable to me... I think I can see both what Maha Maya and what you are saying—you both want me to play my own game. And feel that I must lead my life to whatever extent I can do so, and I accept this. I have no choice but to rely on my inner reserves and the blessings of my elders and well wishers'. I lapsed into silence.

'One of the best ways for an aspiring writer is to think of his life as a script which has to be narrated, if to no one else, then to those who would be interested in his spiritual journey. So it is imperative that his life be made as spiritually interesting as possible and of course one weeds off the non essential points... so the challenge for you is to make your life interesting enough to comment upon by yourself. If your experiences are of little use there will be almost no impetus to write anything about your experiments in spirituality'. I fully concurred with his views, but told him that the external factors in a life were not so important to me. I wanted to make known the psychological bases that could be applied to anyone in his or her life to make it hypnotically interesting and magnificently successful in terms of relationships.

'Outwardly the life of many sages have been very dull and boring, even repetitive to the point of being nauseating. Yet inwardly their experiences have been rich and fabulous. It is this which fascinates me, the adventure of the spirit, a spirit which soars deep and far into inner recesses of being.

'It is in this context that the 'other' which you talk about becomes so fascinating. In the midst of the humdrum of life comes into flower this strange little presence which makes all the pain and suffering redundant and tolerable. It makes of life a spiritual journey that washes away the sins of the physical materiality, but obviously one must be alive to the presence of the 'other', else life will be useless. It is obvious to me now why the goddess sent me to you, she wanted me to hear from you the way she will present herself to me in my life, apart from my gazing practices, which in any case have to be limited to some extent by my constraint on time while living in a city. The 'other' will be the medium through which she will appear to me at many turns of the road, and help me to make something of the loneliness of city life. In the city one cannot survive without the 'other' being present in one's perception and in one's emotional life. Yes, she will come to me in all shapes and sizes—as a child, as a young woman, as a mother, and as an old woman who has seen the ups and downs of life but has remained spiritually intact. I am grateful to you Sri Turiya for opening up this vast domain to me which lay just below the lid of my consciousness but had to be opened somehow so that the revelation of 'otherness' came to me and would remain with me. Yes, you have given me a gift that cannot be surpassed. You have given me spiritual manna which will ensure that in the midst of this human life I am never in want of the 'other' and am always in the company of the goddess. Even though all my companions may be too preoccupied to have time for me the 'other' will manifest in manifold ways and my gazing practices will flourish even more because of it'. I was in tears of gratitude and happiness, and realized that at that moment Sri Turiya had gifted me the secret of life, and that my life would be absolutely worthwhile.

'Don't worry, my friend, you have already paid for your extravagant journey in scores of lives that are past. Now you have been put in chains that cannot allow you to get bogged down in the physical domains of life.

'You will be so fortunate, and these are my blessings, that even while you make your way through the world you will gather strength to fight with the evil forces that come in your path, and fight them decisively. There will be no phyrric victories for you, your victories will always be decisive and complete, and give you great cause for rejoicing. So be glad and do not feel as if you are losing me and Ma. You have to go away so that you live your own life on your own terms, and there is only the goddess and the 'other' for company. Believe me that is more than enough. Your life will be replete with happiness for over scores of past lives you have accumulated the Karma which makes you strong and sensitive to the spiritual journey which is life itself. You do not want more than what you need and that you will get. Be happy my friend for your days on earth are numbered in golden letters. You will never come back, so savor each day as much as you can and give you moments an extravagant flavour, because it's the curtain call for you. You ask me how do I know this and I can only reply that Maha Maya never manifests herself to anyone except when his journey has ended and she is forced to take him to her bosom and push him, boost him into the vast belly of Brahman,. Sri Turiya was overcome with passion and his eyes blazed with emotion. I was silent as I was sure that he was pausing before continuing with his discourse.

It is not as if you will not experience the pain of living, but this will be at an arms length for you and will not come piercing you in your belly. The pain which you had to feel has been felt in previous lives and it is only the pain of existence that will haunt you now,..'

'Even when a man has transcended the mind, and you had pointed this out yourself, there remains the pain that one could not really take others with oneself, that they remain in the Ocean of Illusion, wallowing in the materiality and physicality of it, still believing in pleasure and having faith in the senses, completely convinced that their animal self has nothing that is beyond it at all. These are the materialists, and there are many of them amongst us. Though they may swear by their gods in fact they abuse them every day by the way that they behave. Their desire in this world is to become materially replete with property so that they can go splurge the senses in all sorts of gluttony and greed. Viewing all this, my friend is a painful business, and that's why the sages and would be sages retreat from the mainstream and build their lives in quiet corners of the world where there is less hustle and bustle and the people are simple in their desires and not literally on fire with their cravings. Your basic fight will have to be to stay within the mainstream physically and yet be mentally wholly our of it completely. That, as I read your life, is the final challenge for you, and rightfully so. If one is moving on with the force of one's karma and is never scheduled to return then he must be in full view of anybody and everybody, and be able to share what he has with one and all. This can't happen if you retreat into the mountains. So you will remain in the thick of action...... and may be in the end you will have a few quiet years living somewhere in the mountains or the plains where you can be alone with your thoughts, feelings, and the impressions and expressions of the 'other'?' I had to find out whether that option was viable and open to me. Would I ever live in a mountain retreat, be it even at the end of my life ? I wanted to know about it from Sri Turiya who was a sage with a far reaching vision, and vast powers of prediction.

'This is a question that is dependent on the goddess and on her manifestations to you as the 'other' . If you think that something as vast and important as that can be decided sitting here by me or you then we both are mistaken . My friend your life is no longer your own, but you are here on a goodwill visit, so to speak, to pay off your final debts to friends and foes alike. You are here on serious business and this is not a romantic extravaganza going on. Your spirit means business. It is here encased in the physical and finally as it senses it's freedom around the bend it is gearing up to get back to the fountainhead, and merge with the Almighty Father.. and you talk of going to a retreat ? What do you think you are heading towards? Some kind of poetic departure, or are you still nursing your hang over of being a sage ? My dear friend you are the furthest thing from being a sage or a mystic, although there are glimmerings of both in you. You are simply a man with the good of humanity in his heart, a man who has reached the end of his journey just by treading a common path all along the way. And now the powers that be have come in to help you out and that means that you pay your debts to each and every person that you know. You have to return every single bit of karma and yes there are those who owe you vast sums of karma too. From these you have to collect so that you can continue with your journey without too much discomfort and unease. I cannot stress enough from what you have told me about your meeting with the elusive goddess that this is a final goodbye for you and that is why it is so full of drama, so full of sentiment, nostalgia, elation and ecstasy. It is also full of the residual depression and existential unhappiness and pain. After all you have paid with your karma to experience one final round of what it is to be a man, a man with ordinary likings and longings. Where you depart is the fact that you are obsessed and haunted with the flashes of life as you live it, which tell you that life is passing, passing, ... you will soon be gone forever never to return to the earth to feel the pain and longing, the glory and the ecstasy, ever again. Such a life is indeed glorious but it is essentially tinged with a kind of tragic pathos. Such a man has reached the end and he is just taking a last bow. It is no longer possible for him to turn around and say he doesn't want to enter into the unknown, doesn't want to go into the belly of Brahman and be exhumed in the fire of knowledge' Sri Turiya was absolutely serious, and as I heard him I felt my body go cold and a sweat break out on my forehead. There could be no doubt about what Sri Turiya was telling me. It was something I had felt in my marrow but had never been able to vocalize, to put into words. It was a subliminal knowledge of a final departure of saying goodbye, that kept me out of getting too involved with anyone or anything. I knew somewhere deep within me that this was the void, the end in toto.

'Yet there is a flip side of the coin and I found that it was all too easy to become attracted or attracted to people. It was almost the dying man's attraction to his nurse as the last woman he was likely to be dealing with in his life. I knew I had to balance both these extreme emotions and remain within the norm of detached attachment. In fact I had found that the only way in which one could be prevented from being swept overboard was to keep a lifeboat in the form of detachment ready and in good condition. Many a time I had to sail out of a relationship that went to reef, and was able to survive without much difficulty because I had not put all of myself into it but had retained that essential ten per cent, that would allow me to keep my sanity if something went wrong.

From what Sri Turiya had been saying it was clear

to me that whether I was saying goodbye to the world in general or not, I was certainly spending my last few hours or days at his retreat. Whether he had been hinting at my leaving or saying something in general was not of issue to me. I wanted to leave as I had been saturated by that life in which there was no action, and where one spent one's time meditating for the good of humanity, purifying the spirit and so on. How was it, I told myself that Sri Turiya was not claiming himself to be an enlightened man. Or was I supposed to say this to him. Whatever it was I was up to my ears in this form of spirituality. I yearned for action and I had told Sri Turiya that I wanted to build a house in the hills, and the first question he had asked me was where I would get the funds to do this. I found this to be a ridiculous question as I certainly wasn't banking upon him to put his bit in.

I left the next day for the plains to continue my studies but my plan of building a house in the hills persisted in my mind. As soon as I was able to do so and had collected some money I planned to go out into the hills and buy some land from where I would get a view of the vast hills, mountains and valleys. In my naivete I had thought I could be a writer in the hills; that is to say live off my writing in the hills. It was in this frame of mind that I had ventured out to a little known village some three hours driving distance from Sri Turiya's retreat. Before I had gone there I had taken a brief diversion to the retreat and had found that Sri Turiya had changed beyond measure. He had detached himself from me completely and talked to me as if I were a stranger, or as someone applying for a job.

He asked me questions regarding my plans in a matter of fact manner and retreated into his shell. I found it difficult to relate to him or to Ma. In retrospect I feel that this was perhaps their way of sending me on my way with maximum boost. A feeling that I had no backup and that I had to write my scholarly report and make my house all by myself. I certainly had no moral or economic help from Sri Turiya and had never expected the latter. It came as a shock to me that a man who could be so warm could also be so cold. The Sri Turiya I remember however is the man who was warm and shared his knowledge with me. It took twenty years and more for that warmth to appear again, but that was after Ma had died from a mysterious paralytic disease and Sri Turiya was a much humbled man. I left the retreat early the next morning not sure at all whether I would be able to make anything of the plans that I had set for myself. My problem was that my gazing meditation had itself started becoming erratic and I would only see clouds and luminescent mists in my view when I practiced with a lamp or candle. On the other hand there was every indication that the goddess was stepping literally on my toes and giving me an invaluable moral support. It was no the basis of this rather mysterious and often covert support that I set out on my next spiritual adventure, which was to stay alone in the interior hills and to build a retreat for myself in which I would live as an in—residence writer of fiction and philosophy. This dream was realized, but not for the full duration, and not in the way I had thought it would materialize.

PART TWO

The Conquest of Self

When I left the shelter of the retreat of Sri Turiya it was like starting all over again in the sense that I knew that I would have to put all my theoretical statements to the test and see how my hypotheses worked in real life situations. What I mean by this is that when I left the retreat it was early morning and I knew that whatever shelter it had offered me was now no longer really available to me and it was now a question of do or die. Moreover I had no time and I had decided that I would go into the enterprise as fully as possible. Now I sat in a bus after arranging my scholarly pursuits as neatly as possible, and going in for something over and beyond the data for a thesis, which everyone did anyway. I had met my professor, and I felt he understood the predicament of a young scholar of the new generation. The data for a thesis was just not enough to spend time on simply for the reason that data yields very slowly in a village and one could spend all one's time talking with the villagers realizing from the first moment that knowledgeable sources are extremely scarce, and when they are located they come with riders and corollaries, the nature of which I would not like to discuss here as this is a slightly different story. The crux of the situation was that I was having an excruciating backache and as the bus lurched towards the station nearest to the village I was planning on adopting for purposes of my research on its religion and ritualistic activities, I winced with pain each time the bus hit a bump.

Even at that point of time when it was happening I knew that this was a moment I would never forget in my entire life because everything that followed was delicately perched in my getting to the village without literally collapsing. This pain was to recur in an accentuated form later in the village and I would be forced to pace the fields in agony. To the best of my knowledge mystic coils of dammed energy were slowly but deliberately surfacing. It took a good week of excruciating pain in the lower back for the pain to stabilize. I have never experienced such aesthetically excruciating pain before or hence. However it left a certain seed of clarity and spirituality in my intellect and mind which has continued to grow ever since.

I wondered in my mind what the village would be like and what the surrounding areas would look like aesthetically speaking. During those days how a place looked and how it felt like were very important to me. I felt that if I liked the place then all would go well. When I reached the village I saw there were a few shops and that the main area of the village market was just a brief stopover for the traveller to further parts of the area. Somehow I got down from the bus mindful of my bad back and got a coolie to get off my trunk and bags. An army truck going upwards took my baggage to the room where I would be staying. I had fixed all that during a previous visit. It was a 'just workable' proposition with an open air lavatory and a tap on either side of it and my room on top of a cowshed. The mud floor of the room had holes in it through which the flies came up in hordes. In fact I remember a day when I was still to settle in when hordes of flies settled on me as I lay down and I couldn't even see an inch of my pyjama !

Although I had been to the village on a previous visit and had visited it during my early student years I had not really got a chance to view it properly. But here even in the midst of my agonizing backache I could clearly see that the village was cradled in scenic beauty with a lovely view of the ice mountains and beautiful valleys stretching wave upon wave till the bottom of the great mountains which rose high and majestic like a cosmic crystal ball. A crystal ball which had probably been held in the perception of the great sages of Sanatana dharma as they contemplated the mysteries of the infinite universe. I felt like a child cradled in their immensity and felt acutely the vast fraility of my mortality. Indeed everytime I looked at the ice mountains it was as if I was looking at my mortality. The great mountains were telling me to use my time well and judiciously, because I was here to go, while they were here to stay. I had always loved the beautiful green mountains since my childhood exposure to them, but I had always been deprived of a face to face encounter with the ice mountains. And now when I saw them with a few wisps of cloud around their summits I had a dying wish...I wished with all my heart and soul that I would be granted a few years with them in solitude or like minded company before the end of my days. This was because I knew the phantasmagorical views that I would have of these mountain deities would not suffice to satiate my appetite to be among their beauty but only whet it further. I also knew that there was no practical way for me to stay in the vicinity and benediction of those mountain deities because like everyone else I had to earn a living and this was possible for me only through my writing. At that point one of my books was under publication and two novels had been published. But I lacked the savvy to market myself and it gradually became clear to me when I had left Devagiri to report to the University that it would not be possible to live on my writing. I was getting next to nothing for it and perhaps had only myself to blame. My dream of living my life in Devagiri lingered and tortured me for many years especially when tensions mounted for me in Delhi. I constantly thought of running to Devagiri but it was obvious to me that nothing would come of it. I had gone to Devagiri for a purpose and once that was over it was no longer tenable to be there. My dream of being a 'writer' had collapsed, in the sense that I would have to do a university job to support myself.

These thoughts were only in the background at that time and what was important to me at that juncture was to put my room together so that I could survive in it without going utterly demented. Apart from the flies and the lowing of cattle in the room below I had to take out my cooker and start preparing food since my stomach was sensitive to the food in the market and I could not imagine myself going there each meal time. I had no funds to employ someone to do my cooking. My landlord was a man of middle height, whom I call Kaptan Saab. He was a bit of an enigma and stayed alone on the first floor of a large hill house, cooking for himself and roaming the village with his brown bhotia dog in the daytime. He offered to share his kitchen with me but I had problems since I was a vegetarian and he ate meat.

I got to work on the room a few days after I had recovered my breath and put wire mesh on the three window spaces. However the door remained a vulnerable point from which the ever present flies managed to creep in. There was a humorous moment when one day I was despairing over these irritating pests. Kaptan Saab walked in with a loud greeting. He had a fly swat in his hand and methodically swatted the flies one by one, sometimes three in one swipe. I laughed uproariously at his determined look and enquired where he had got that swat from, and he said that it was available in the District town, where Sri Turiya also lived. I made a note that the next time I went there I would get one myself, meanwhile the Kaptan said he would leave it for me to use. With simple gestures like these the Kaptan won my trust and confidence. Having almost totally lost contact with Sri Turiya and in the midst of a crisis of confidence regarding how to locate a person who knew about the religion ritual and general culture of the area Kaptan Saab came to me as a god send. I found his sense of wry humour and his lifestyle of cooking for himself and living alone very appealing. In fact from the smoke stained windows of his huge balcony on the first floor of the house adjacent to my room was a fabulous view of the eternal snows. I had mentioned to Kaptan Saab that if we cleaned those windows to a shiny translucence we would literally have those eternal snows right beside us. 'That's why', said Kaptan Saab 'I have let them become a bit dusty and smoky. These mountains are hard to live with and I have been here almost twenty years, living in their presence'.

'Why should it be hard? I think it's a privilege to be in their presence all the time...they are reminders of our glorious heritage and mentioned in almost every religious text, old or new'. I was much taken aback that Kaptan Saab could think of downplaying their beauty and presence by letting his windows gather smog.

'These mountains are very powerful, and if a man does not measure upto perfection, which their presence demands, one can tend to feel very depressed. Not many local people would like to stare at them the way you do. This is not because they do not revere them but because they feel that one must not look straight at the gods and goddesses that live amongst them. You say you would like to live amongst them always, but that is a matter for the great mountain gods and goddesses to decide. They may have something else in mind for you!' Kaptan Saab looked me in the eye. 'Do not worry too much about the future, and as regards your work I will ensure that you get your material. Let me give you the key to one of the facts that I have discovered my self – the world of spirit is a replica of all there is in the material world! Everything that is here is there!' Kaptan Saab was emphatic. I sensed this was not a debatable issue, it was a matter of total belief.

'Do you mean that this house, my room, these trees, and the great mountains are all there?' I was incredulous. I could hardly believe what I was hearing.

'Everything!' said Kaptan Saab. 'The only problem is that you can neither add anything or discard anything. Everything you have in this world will be there in the other world when you die, but you won't be able to add anything ' or to throw anything away'. Kaptan Saab was not being frivolous. He spoke in the tone of a man who knows. We dropped the conversation there and I thanked him for letting me in on something that I felt had more value for me as a person than anything to do with my work and research as such.

My first concern apart from my research work was to find a piece of land with a beautiful view of the grand ice mountain ranges. I had expressed this to Kaptan Saab, and to the various people I met. I had asked them to let me know if there was any land available for building a hut for myself. In those days I fancied myself to be a classical anthropologist in the budding. I felt that I would need a field headquarters, from where to conduct my future, even lifetime research, in rural religion and spirituality.

I scarcely realized that my dream headquarters would start materializing within a few weeks and that building the house would become a key ingress to the life of the construction workers in that area. These workers do different kinds of jobs, like quarrying stone, masonry, carpentry, laying slates on the roof of the house and so on. I developed deep friendships with these wonderful people during my stay there. Living in the midst of their hardships, having scarcely a pair of clothes to live in they were perennially cheerful. They shared whatever they knew with me, and invited me to their rituals. I was made to feel like an honoured guest which really embarrassed me, but they were adamant on giving me love, respect and honour. I cherish their wonderful and humane attitude today, and feel that if their spirit of cheerfulness and resilience could be inculcated world wide there would really be a global renaissance. To me the exposure to these wonderful people was a benediction, something that I can only be grateful for.

During the first few weeks at Devagiri I had very few distractions, and in the evenings I would climb up the hill and sit on a crescent shaped field and look out into the valley, trying out my spiritual practice of gazing, while looking at the snows. Many a time the ice mountains were not out but covered in cloud and since my practice was basically focused around a lamp I had little success initially. When I got a bit used to it I found that if one gazed at a certain point in the vast range of snows the whole scenery gradually disappeared in the glow of a throbbing golden light. There was nothing and I felt as if I was myself dissolved into the light. The important secret of this type of gazing was to keep the eyes from blinking too much. If one could hold them from blinking the world became one of golden light.

After dinner which I cooked for myself in the cooker over a kerosine stove I would recline and attempt gazing by focussing toward a candle. It was this practice which really buoyed me up since I could catch a glimpse of Maya almost each time I meditated. Yet in those early sessions though I saw her it was as if she were busy doing something and did not want to talk. Having heard her at the remote temple, and having evidence that she was indeed the soul of every woman I did not mind this silence. In fact I knew this was a prelude to further conversations with her some of which I could report almost verbatim. Meanwhile I realized that by her silence Maya did not want to begin a conversation with me directly and I guessed she wanted me to interact further with Kaptan and the villagers. I realized that this gesture on her part was very gracious since I tended to get obsessed with her and her words very easily. If I had lengthy conversations with her without sufficient information about my situation it would be of no use. Maya by her reticence was obviously encouraging me to talk to Kaptan Saab and the villagers. This is exactly what I had in mind and at the same time I had picked up enough of Maya's silent tongue, or the language of kinesthetics and gesture to be able to read her actions as if they were words in a book. This is not to say that I did not look forward each evening after dinner to gaze into a dimly lit candle and to watch her speak with simple actions and gestures. I knew enough about her silent language to realize that she wanted me to go ahead with trying to find and buy some land on which to build a hut. That is all I really wanted to know from her at that stage apart from having her gorgeous presence in the enthralling beauty of the mountains, snows, trees and the lovely blue skies. I felt that I had reached heaven, and this time not in my gazing but in the world of actual and social perception.

Sometimes Kaptan Saab would invite himself to my evening walk up the main path leading to the higher end of the village. He would suggest areas along that path where he could get me some land for my hut. There were a few areas available but the problem of water and the view always seemed to loom large and cut down on his suggestions. One day Kaptan Saab suggested that he had just right place for me, a place which had the vast stretch of snow mountains bang in front of it, and where water could be made available relatively easily. Also it was 'central' so far as the village area was concerned.

'What is this place you are talking about Kaptan Saab?' I asked with much curiosity since I had seen almost the entire village.

'It is the field on which you sit almost every evening and look over the valley!' he said with a voice that rang with finality. He had made his final offer and I was free to take it or leave it.

'That's alright'. I said, 'but how much is it going to cost me?'

I wanted the economics to be right since I didn't have an endless bank account to play with. In fact the cost of the land was every single penny I would have on me for the next year. Yet I was deeply infatuated with that field and with the panoramic view of the snows. I would have given all I had to put a hut on it and live there. I told Kaptan Saab that I had only postdated cheques with me and that I could pay the amount only in about an year.

It was mutually decided that I pay a certain sum to indicate my intention to buy that land and that I was to pay a certain amount each month until the total was complete. It was also written down on the government stamp paper that if I failed to pay the total amount before the stipulated date, I would forfeit the entire amount that had been paid previously.

The actual writing of the document was done in my little room and the table was my trunk! At the time of signing the document I had to declare in writing that I was transacting the deal 'in full knowledge, awareness, and consciousness', and that I was fully responsible and committed to the deal. Little did I know then that I had signed my own warrant so far as the research work was concerned. Throughout that interminably long stay in Devagiri whenever the chips were down I thought of taking the first bus back to Delhi, and calling it a day. The fact that I had paid money for a piece of land and wanted to build a hut on it put a severe brake on this type of thinking from materializing. I had put such a brake on my movements that there was no possibility of even changing my address from Devagiri to some other village. This was because in the span of about an year I had already changed two addresses. My professor in Delhi would get hopping mad if I did that and I felt it would be totally unfair for me to behave irresponsibly. Moreover I had already got a sniff of the spirituality of the area and that too kept me from abandoning my trail. The fact, as I saw it was that spirituality, religion and ritual in that area, at least, if not the entire region needed to be documented before the talons of civilization took over and buried everything below a cultural onslaught from other hill towns and also from the plains.

In effect all my cash had been located to buy the land and I felt that I could manage something to keep the kitchen going. I had no idea from where I would get money for the hut and considered even building one of those village shanties made of stone and straw. Meanwhile I busied myself with work and started mingling with the people whom I found to be generous intelligent, witty and very committed to Sanatana dharma. In fact one of the stupidest questions I had kept asking for more than an year met its answer in Devagiri. I was sitting drinking tea at a shop, when I asked the shopkeeper.

'What is the religion of the people here ?' I was still puzzled over an year of research.

'We are Hindus, our religion is not different from that of the Hindus of the plains' He looked at me somewhat amused.

I was much taken aback at his candor and my own stupidity. For over an year I had been confusing the different forms of Hinduism and had almost become quite sure that I was studying the rituals of a 'different' religion. I would say that this was a serendipitous moment in my research'. Meanwhile another interesting development had started taking place so far as religion and spirituality is concerned. One morning I had been taking tea in the down market tea stall when a ochre robed long haired mendicant had entered. I am normally wary of such people because sometimes they see no further than your pocket. But this individual was different. After exchanging our introductions. Baba Tambari, as he called himself, announced he was touring the entire District raising funds for a Siva Temple to be built on the spur opposite the market where the foundations had already been laid by the villagers. He didn't ask me for a donation but we shared good vibrations, and liked each other. Throughout my stay in Devagiri I would often meet Baba Tambari and we would talk a bit while we looked deep into the snows. On occasions that we met on the field that I was buying Baba would exclaim and say 'give me some place on this field to put up my hut, it is truly beautiful'. Baba was a busy man and wholly committed to building the temple and he was often travelling, collecting money, and spending it on the construction of the temple. An amusing incident took place in this regard. The villagers had all decided to give some money for the construction of the temple. Everyone except for Kaptan Saab had given whatever they could. When Baba Tambari asked Kaptan Saab why he wasn't giving the money as it was certainly not too much he answered that the temple was opposite to a girls school and once the temple was made all sorts of sadhus and mendicants would come there. This according to Kaptan Saab would be a bad influence on them. He stuck to this stand for a day or two but later relented and gave his donation.

Having no source of funds or a bank balance I had no alternative but to take my parents into confidence regarding what I had done and what my plans were. I was surprised to receive a cordial and affectionate reply within a matter of days. My parents said they were happy for me and that they wanted to see the piece of land that I was in the process of purchasing. Later in the month of June 1980, they came to Devagiri to see the piece of land that I had fancied and made the deal for. Kaptan was with us when I showed them the field on a lovely sunny day with clouds in the sky like fluffs of cotton. My father a very astute and practical army Brigadier liked the piece of land but had two very pertinent questions to ask Kaptan: where would the water come from and where was the nearest electricity connection. After being shown these points were quite close by my father felt that I had behaved sensibly by not planning to buy a piece of land that would not have any water or electricity. Under such conditions living in the hills can become a very trying and difficult situation. My parents and myself decided that we would buy the whole field rather than leave a tail end which could cause problems later. The person who owned the field named a price, and we reluctantly agreed because in those days all these prices were exorbitant sums, but we agreed to pay the fancy prices because we liked the view and the location of the field. The result was that the entire field was purchased at one go with a cheque that my parents sent me when they went back to Delhi. That left me tc deal with the field all on my own, as it should be.

By now I had started attending regularly some of the local rituals of divination as a follow up to work done earlier on exorcist rituals. I had also begun making friendships with the people of the area and had got the village legend from them. However my work went hand in hand with my work for the house that I wanted to build. My father was against the idea that I spend some money and make a hut – a single room to live in. He felt that I should go in for a small bungalow type of construction, with a huge covered verandah, large windows, high doors, slate roof, and a floor laid with slates. This would make it a house which was not exactly traditional to the area but a modern one which would suit our needs, we felt in later times, when we needed it during the summer or during some project in that area.

This meant that I had now to register the land in my name, once the money had been paid, and I did this with a heavy heart. There was no one from my side in that taxi which took us to the District Headquarters to register the land in my name. It was an emotional feeling for me to be 'alone' in the taxi with four other locals. The work in the town was done rather slowly and many pages had to be typed and signed. Later it was found that there was something wrong with the papers and when my father came in October he was kind enough to help me sort matters out in the town and complete the formalities. As must be obvious I was still only beginning to find my feet in the world of men, though in the world of spirit I was far more confident about myself.

Meanwhile a cataclysmic event had occurred in my spiritual life in the month of July. I had found that gazing in the small room that I was living in, and after having cooked food myself was very difficult. I was hardly able to muster up the relevant energy and direction. However goddess Maya appeared in an early morning dream in July in which I saw myself standing, and then leaping off a cliff. That day it began raining and was deeply cast over. The mountains looked gloomy and as I sat on my cot in the room wondering what I should do, a knock came on the door. I went to open the door and saw one of my local friends smiling at me. I asked him to come in and sit down, but he said that he was in a hurry and that several other young men were waiting for us.

'What's the matter, where are we going?' I asked him somewhat perplexed by his hurry and excitement. Normally my village friends were quite casual about timings.

'We are going to the collective exorcism where only a few villagers are selected to go ... and the headman has asked you to come with us as this happens only once in two years'. My villager friend was clearly somewhat impatient.

'Alright', I said, ' give me a mınute'.

I put on my shoes and arranged my sling bag, and picked up my umbrella, as the rain had worsened. I locked my room and we went down the road towards the market. There were just the two of us, and I wondered aloud about the others.

'They have gone ahead of us and will meet us in the next village', said my friend. There was hardly anyone on the street that day as it was raining and we walked down the path for a few kilometre's before sighting the village. This village had even then, in 1980, been fully converted to modernism. The huts in that village were made of concrete and so also the roofs. The joints of these new village huts were smeared with tarmacadum. I got quite a nasty surprise, when I saw these buildings, but did not ask what it was all about. Yet the villager friend I had with me said that this was the new trend in the region. The slate roofs and the tin roofs were being now replaced with concrete. To my eyes they did not merge with the mountains but stood out as if something had been picked up and stuck in there.

From that village onwards the path started to climb and was very slippery. Also the distance that had to be covered in those damp and rainy conditions meant that we had to walk on for another eight to ten hours, which meant we would get there only in the late evening. There were another seven members to our party, and including us that meant we were nine. We took along with us two goats and everyone carried rations. The planned stay was about a week and all our rations would have to be carefully used. The goats too were to be sacrificed to the deities of the temple of the exorcists, and then eaten as a sacrament. The young men were also to gather certain medicinal herbs found only in that area. I kept up the conversation with them.

'Where exactly are we going?' I asked through the rain.

'There are two small plateaus', the leader replied. He must have been in his early thirties.

'Okay!', I said , 'Tell me some more about them'.

'The story is that they were formed when there was a mighty earthquake in Vedic times. The first series of jolts formed the Lower Plateau, while the more drastic jolts pushed up the mountain into the Higher Plateau. Ever since we hill folk have come to Devagiri we have to come to do a week long penance in the Lower and Higher Plateaus for the safety of the village and the entire region. We who have come have been selected from among the exorcist groups who have danced around the sacred fire at the local exorcist village level meetings. This is a serious responsibility that has been given to us'. The exorcist leader looked at me to see if I was following the drift of his talk.

'How come I was allowed to be with you and participate in this series of exorcist rituals? Who was responsible for letting me come to it. Obviously this is the first time that anyone has been allowed apart from the villagers themselves?' I was a bit puzzled, and though elation rose and suppressed my panic, I was by now getting to feel that I might not last out the week on a high mountain plateau, at least 9000 feet above sea level bang opposite the ice ranges, running freezing temperatures.

' It was the headman of the village who said that you could come with us and he felt that you would never understand the exorcist rituals unless you attended this one. Further it was Kaptan Saab who said he had promised to let you in on information that would tie up your research work. This ritual happens once in two years and you would not be here the next time. If you missed this opportunity then what you would be presenting about exorcism would be a partial and distorted picture.' The leader stopped talking and the path was getting a bit level after hours of steep rocky climbing. I was panting out of breath by the time we touched level ground again with packed mud on it.

'We are approaching the Lower Plateau', shouted one of our party, and there were innumerable little hillside coves with statues of Lord Ganesh in them, in which some passing worshipper had placed a leaf or a flower as part of the worship. The rain had eased off though there was no sun and a thin mist blowing like incense smoke, making the entire valley and hillside have a haunting appeal.

'We will rest and pray in the temple for an hour', said my friend.

'It is late,' said the exorcist leader. It may be better to sleep in the temple area today and carry on tomorrow. What do you say? He had put the question to no one in general. There was no one to argue with this casual sounding decision, but it was understood that no one was to go against the directions of the leader. So confident was he of his authority that he did not even have to assert himself and his voice had barely been audible'

I couldn't have welcomed this halt at the Siva Kali temple more since it came after at least six hours of walking with only a little food along the way. Here in the temple we would get some nice hot food and a place to rest for the night. We would reach the Higher Plateau late in the afternoon. There would be enough time to organize ourselves. I was especially keen to have a long conversation with the Bhagavad Baba who lived there all alone around the year. I sincerely wondered how he did that though there were occasion's that he would come down to the Lower Plateau. That was as far as he would go, and no further towards civilization. I really did not want to meet him in a pedestrian state of mind and therefore I welcomed the break. The priest of the temple came out of his room when he heard us ringing the temple bells. It was late evening and there was a spectacular sunset across the mountains, a good and auspicious sign.

The priest was a middle aged man who looked after the temple and had a couple as his assistants. Our group was given a hot glass of tea along with some prasad (sweets) to eat which we welcomed since we were tired walking all day in the rain which had now stopped. We all had a darshan of the Siva and Kali statues and gave some offerings to them as the priest lit the evening oil lamps around the area which cordoned off the statues. The members of our party helped the couple who assisted the priest to prepare the evening meal after which came the prayer to the deities comprising the singing of sacred songs and performing s worship of the deities with the oil lamps moving in circles around the statues. We had the simple meal and went to bed early in the building opposite the temple which had rooms for travellers to the Lower Plateau, or the rare visitors to the Higher Plateau. The priest had already told us in the evening that the army was cordoning off the Higher Plateau with barbed wire and that the work on this had already begun.

'There will be no next time, for your group', he told the leader 'because the work to prevent anyone going to the Higher Plateau has already begun'.

'What about the Bhagavad Baba?' asked the leader 'How will he come and go in the change of seasons?'

'Well Baba knows this mountain area better than a goat, and the pilgrim route which leads to an almost dead end at the Higher Plateau, is one of several routes up to the final approach to the Higher Plateau. Ordinary pilgrims cannot take those paths, they are too steep and dangerous, compared to the regular route which is treacherous itself, especially in the rain'. The priest seemed perturbed at the impending closure of the pilgrim route , but what seemed to disturb him greatly was the fact that they would soon start building barracks a little beyond the temple and a small contingent of soldiers would remain throughout the year in that area. But he was a circumspect man and he refrained from talking too much about his reactions.

My gazing meditation that night after the meal was very sketchy as I was feeling sleepy. So after a few attempts at trying to focus on the lamps in the temple I thought the better of it and went to sleep in the room opposite the temple where another of my companions was. I lay down on the mattress and went to sleep and almost immediately I entered into a lucid dream. I was standing beside the gorgeous goddess Maya who was sitting on a large rock near a stream with crystal waters . She was clad in a pink sari with silver frills and had her long hair loose. She was smiling at me in a restrained way and my heart was thumping. It had been a long time, by my standards since the goddess had looked me in the eye and I was thrilled beyond measure. In fact all my gazing practices had not yielded much by way of her eye contact or words and hence I was overjoyed when she spoke to me.

'Well, you are now far away from Sri Turiya, and he has played his part in your life. I did not want to come in and talk to you in words for two reasons: one is that you tend to get extremely elated, and the other is that you have a tendency to lethargy when you talk to me. I wanted to wait long enough so that you could be relatively 'normal', while being in my presence and conversing with me. Tonight I have chosen a somewhat better approach to you in your dreams because you are too exhausted to gaze into the flames. I want to tell you that the experiences that you are going to have at the Higher Plateau are such that they will never be repeated, either for you or for anyone else. Further the holy man (Bhagavad Baba) who lives there himself has a few years to live there since once the area is cordoned off he would have to chose some other place to live. My understanding is that rather than do that he would take Mahasamadhi there after a few years as he is already quite old and to move somewhere else would not be feasible. Throughout his life Baba has taught aspects of Sanatana Dharma to the exorcists from Devagiri and to a few pilgrims who are his devotees. The army will give him his rations, but as you know the real purpose of life for a holy man is to disseminate what he has learned. He will then make devotees of the army soldiers and they will benefit by his wisdom. But as I told you Baba is in his last years and this is a good opportunity for you to talk to him about all aspects of whatever you want to know. So let the exorcists do their worship, and gather your notes in the evening when they have finished. After witnessing the first round of activities be selective about what you are going to witness since it is repetitive. I understand these ceremonies will help you piece together the exorcist puzzle, but your larger, long term job is to sit at Baba's hut and talk to him for as long as possible. This has to be done especially in the early evening and into the night. These are the times that Baba meditates, but now that he is a old man he would not mind sharing his perceptions, which you in turn, could share with those who are interested. This would be something of a truly religious nature rather than being something of 'research' value alone. I have not come into your dream for a conversation, that is something now you have to reserve for Baba, and you are at liberty to discuss your conversations with me with the Baba, who is a man of vast experience. He won't find you odd, and remember he has met many types of devotees in his life. So feel free to be yourself and do not try to conform to some 'type' of devotee. I would urge you to be relaxed and free and ask him a few central questions, which are at the same type simple, so that when you ultimately share these conversations they are for the devotees in general and not for your classmates who would like something abstract and obstruse. Baba already has a tendency to be complicated, so don't ask questions which would make the situation get out of hand. I don't want your conversations with Baba to be a mockery of Sanatana Dharma which is essentially a way of doing things in the 'right' way which leads to happiness and bliss both here and hereafter.'

As I watched the goddess turned into a pinkish mist which twirled and became a carnation flower. Maya was no longer there. I left the flower growing in a niche of the rock and as I turned to go I woke up suddenly. There were great rolls of thunder, and another thundershower was obviously building up. I was sure that there would be a rough climb for us the next day. I recapitulated to myself what the goddess Maya had said to myself and felt bliss suffuse every pore of my being. Having seen her after a long while face to face and having heard her exquisite voice I was back in the womb of bliss. I lay thinking about her and visualizing her simple yet beautiful face and suddenly blinked off into a deep and restful slumber, feeling very, very happy.

We all woke up early in the morning and had a bath in the ice cold water which literally jerked me awake. This had been my practice in the mountains every morning. I was used to having a cold water bath and found this was an excellent way to wake up. After the intense cold there was an after wave of warmth all over the body tingling with freshness. We ate our meal after offering the food to the deities and started out towards the Higher Plateau in the semi-darkness. The words of Maya devi were fresh in my mind and suddenly the focus had shifted for me from the exorcist rituals alone to the Bhagavad Baba. Further the priest had given a few kilograms of ration to each of us to offer to the Baba and we were walking amidst a shower of rain on slippery paths which wound upwards towards the Higher Plateau.

Because of the rain and mist amidst which we walked there was hardly anything that we could see. It was important that each step be taken carefully and on occasion each one of us had slipped on the slimy clay on the paths. I was using my umbrella less to protect myself from the incessant rain than to poke its sharp head into the slimy mud so that I would not slip.After several hours of walking in which we kept up cheer and our spirits by shouting and talking loudly to each other we finally reached the stretch which gave the mountain it's name. This was a vast stretch of land on which there was no vegetation and was relatively flat, but undulating. The rain had stopped and the mist swirled like a crazy dervish all around us.We were 9000 feet above sea level and virtually in no man's land.The pilgrims who came here were few and far between and they had to be very keen to meet the sage of the Higher Plateau because that was the end of the journey. There was no route that led out of the spur. One had to go back on the track and retrace one's steps back to the Lower Plateau. We walked on the shale like rock terrain until we reached the end of this flatland high up in the mountains. Beyond that was a deep fall of over a thousand feet, and the only way to reach the spur on which the temple was located, was to climb down a huge rock on which there were literally vertical foot and handholds. One mistake meant a free fall of over a thousand feet into the heavily forested valley down below.

I watched the leader say his prayers before going down the rock face which must have been at least twenty feet in length. He then slung his belongings around his neck and took a rope and tied it to an outcrop of rocks. He then went down gingerly face towards the rock and soon we heard he had reached the ground below. He gave a triumphant shout and gave a tug on the rope. One by one we all went over the edge and down on firm ground below which was still slippery from the rain of the last few days. The last man tied the goats one by one and sent them over the rock bleating piteously. As it is they had a few days to live before the exorcists offered them to the gods and ate them as sacramental food, which would ward off evil from the party and the entire village which was by now some three thousand feet below us. The exorcist leader told me that on a clear day one could see the village Devagiri from the temple on the spur of the High Plateau, and assured me that the entire area around it appeared to be completely flat due to the discrepancy in the height which would be over three thousand feet.

I had imagined that the worst was over and had fully realized why this temple was not exactly on the pilgrim route.It was trecherously located. Below the rock the land was full of yellowish muddy clay and one's feet slipped and slithered about. I found that my umbrella point was no match for the slime that was there all around. The leader advised that we catch the creepers from the trees around and go from shrub to shrub. I had a most nasty moment when I lost control and slipped and went slithering at top speed towards the precipice. I just managed to brake in time, which was fortunate for me since the chance of surviving a fall from that mountain side into the valley below was very dim if not non existent. Finally after slithering in the wet clay and taking many near tumbles I reached the stony path that led to the top of the temple on the spur. It was a small area there some fifty feet by fifty feet, maybe a little more, and towards the western side was a small temple of Siva and Kali embossed on a marble bust which had been brought there generations earlier by the exorcists of Devagiri, who were still on the traditional path of warding off collective evils on the village by placating their most important deities through specific rituals dedicated to them.

We all had a profound moment when we genuflected before the deities and lit incense and oil lamps before the icons. I truly felt as if some supernatural force had saved me both at the rock face and later in the slippery cliff edge full of wet clay. I vowed to myself that I would try to live up to this second lease in life by doing my best in whatever life faced me with. I could see that the others, all exorcists were undergoing profound moments themselves, and probably praying to the deities. I could only guess at this because these moments were too private and too precious to be violated by anthropological curiosity.

I would like to take a brief detour here, at the point where we have reached the Holy Temple at the top of the High Plateau. It concerns the anthropological curiosity. Perhaps I have missed crucial data in my previous anthropological work because I felt there was a 'private zone' that should not be crossed by the anthropologist. There is something sacred in every human being and every human situation which should not be profaned . It is however quite the practice to bulldoze into the most delicate of situations and ask the most thick skinned of questions. These questions are not even delicately put but literally thrown on a person who may be undergoing an intensely private moment of sorrow, despair, elation or bliss. The attempt to make these moments public property must be reversed in every writing profession be it literature, anthropology or others. I also maintain that beyond a point science and religion have to remain good friends but cannot become close relatives. This is because the soul of man cannot be dissected and quantified by machines and microscopes.

After I had got my breath back in a minute I found that the small flat spur on the High Plateau was washed by swirling mists and winds. I literally felt scared that I might get blown off into the precipitous falls which were three sides of the spur, easing a bit only on the western side where a thin vegetated ridge ran flatly towards a distant district town which we could see far away. I certainly could not recognize it but the exorcist leader told me that on a clear day one could see some obvious landmarks by which one could place the town quite definitely.

It had rained again and my clothes were soaking wet and it was so cold that I tried to light a fire. I asked where the Baba was and told that he was busy in his hut about thirty feet below to the north of the temple. I was freezing but all the wood was wet. I now realized the wisdom of carrying kerosine along with the rations and soon we got to the Lower Temple where the entire party was to stay during the night. The previous party which had come had left a large tree trunk to dry for the next group and we splintered wood off it with an axe that one of the exorcists had brought along specifically for this purpose.

Then came the problem of water. There was a spring some hundred feet below from which the water was brought up in buckets and used for drinking and cooking purposes. A fire was started with the wet wood after it was splashed with kerosine. At the same time the huge trunk of the tree was shifted gradually so that it would start to burn. The glass of tea that I had in that mountain temple high up in the ranges was perhaps the most welcome beverage that I have ever had. My shock was now receding and all of us shared moments of happiness and camaraderie. The capacity of that mountain setting to provide refreshment to the human spirit was beyond belief. I felt as if I was flying through the air, so rarified was the air and I felt like shouting out loud and singing and dancing. In retrospect I do not think it was the air alone that set off a blissful trajectory for the psyche. I think it had everything to do with the sacredness of the temples which had been sanctified by the ages and made one feel that one would never get back to civilization alive.It felt as if those were the last moments of one's life and this set off a feeling of both sobriety as well as blissfulness in all of us.

Members of the exorcist party had already built a fire and we all huddled around it trying to warm ourselves and trying to dry our clothes. It was deep evening and we had had a grueling journey up to the spur. However I learned from the leader of the exorcists that the night was to be spent in chanting and singing sacred songs in praise of the deity. This decision surprised me very much since by all logic the exorcists should have been eager to feed themselves and have a good nights sleep. It was somewhat disappointing for me also that Bhagavad Baba would not be available till the next morning as he spent time in his meditation at night. I could not but help marvel at the grit and sincerity of these young mountain exorcists. Their spirit of worship was second to none. It gave me the energy to shake off my tiredness and participate at least in the chanting of mantras and then partake of the sanctified food before I watched them sing the sacred songs with great fervor. I felt greatly elated at being on this lonely inaccessible mountain temple alone with a small band of spiritually inclined young men who were placating the gods on behalf of all the villagers. Once the sacred songs had been sung we retired to the lower temple house which served as a night shelter. It was very low and I had to bend almost double to get into it. The fire was now lit and the tree trunk had begun burning. I was given a stone slab near the temple and stretched out on it almost unconscious, so tired was I after the days trek. It crossed my mind that we were virtually cut off from civilization and I had fears as to how we were going to get back safe and sound.

I tried to sleep, and it occurred to me that if I shifted suddenly almost half my body would crash into the embers and low flames of the sacred fire. But I was too tired. I fell off to a half sleep and soon found that there was a burning sensation in my legs. Yet when I looked down my legs were away from the flames. When I lay down again this fiery sensation spread from my legs upwards until I felt as if I was upon a funeral pyre. There was a sensation of low heat all over my body and I was too paralyzed by exhaustion to move from my position. I sincerely believed I had died and was being cremated. As this burning sensation turned to a gentle warmth I fell asleep and woke only when the exorcists were going down in pairs to get water from the spring and to bathe in the ice cold water in preparation for the days exorcist rituals. I did not tell anyone of my experience with the fire that night but was determined to talk it over with Bhagavad Baba when I got the opportunity to do so. The goats had been tied to stakes and chewed on the grass that grew on and near the spur. When I asked the leader why they didn't let them loose he told me that mountain goats are very nimble and could quite easily get lost in the surrounding area.

I went with one of the younger exorcists to the spring which had a firm path to it and after much hesitation poured a bucket of ice cold water over my head. I screamed out loud as the water washed over my body. It was ice cold and I started shivering almost immediately. The exorcists reaction was to burst out into merriment and laughter. However I found that soon a sensation of pleasant warmth began to flow in me. I was fully awake. When I had gathered my clothes and was turning to go back up the path I was face to face with a hoary old man who was dark and wore nothing but a loincloth. As is the custom of the region I immediately touched his feet. The old man was Bhagavad Baba.

'So you have come at last', said the old man brushing back his grey beard with a flourish. 'I have been waiting for you for a long time! Good! Have something to eat and come to my hut. I disappointed you last night but for the next few days and nights you can come to my hut whenever you have the time. Do not neglect your work, but remember that it is ultimately your encounter with me that will make the difference'.

'Can I help you with your bath ? Shall I pour the water over you?' I asked with great enthusiasm. The Baba had a most cheerful voice and it was obvious that years of solitude had brought him to his goal of Moksa, spiritual liberation.

'No, no, my son', said Bhagavad Baba 'If I allow you

to do that, the very next request you will make is to let you stay with me on this mountain top'. He laughed uproariously. I was much taken aback because exactly that feeling was taking shape in my mind. In those days I was a desperately eager young man so far as spiritual matters went and I wanted to retire from the world with any holy man who was living reclusively.

'How did you know that I was going to ask you that?' I asked in growing perplexion.

'It is written all over your countenance', said Baba. 'But don't worry, what you want to know is how one is to live in the world of men and remain at peace in one's heart. That and more I will be able to tell you. You are here for a number of days, and believe me time slows down on this mountain top. It goes according to the watch in my mind. I will not let you or the exorcists go until you are yourself happy to do so! Are you satisfied?' The Baba playfully tweaked my left ear and I laughed loudly at his gesture.

We climbed at bit upward on the path and watched the Baba do his ablutions. He sat directly under the ice cold spring water and cleaned himself with a little sandstone he had brought with himself. It was obvious that he was enjoying himself and that the temperature of the water was just right for him. He dried himself with a thin piece of fabric which he had brought with himself and filled up his brass bucket with the spring water.

'Go eat something my dear friend', he said, 'And then come to my hut in about an hour. I'll be through with my morning meditation by then'. I did not say a word. A quiet ecstasy was burning within my chest and my heart was pounding as if it would burst. Just being with Bhagavad Baba for that brief duration and hearing him speak in that cheerful blissful tone had left me speechless. I walked up the path as if there were springs in my feet such was the pounding energy in my body. I ate the sanctified food in silence and then asked what was the exorcists' plan for the day.

'We are going to oblate the deities and do chanting during the day. In the afternoon we will meditate on the mantra of the deities, and in the evening there will be sacred songs. I told them that I would watch them begin the worship and then go to Bhagavad Baba, if they did not mind.

'We have brought you here to meet Baba, apart from seeing what we are doing. This was the plan of the headman as soon as he heard your questions. Questions to which Bhagavad Baba has the right answers. He will change your life. He will sow the seeds of happiness and joy in you. Seeds that will burst forth into bloom many years later when you need the fruits of wisdom the most.. Right now you think of nothing but the house you are building and how you will complete your work for the University. A time will come when you will have to face the whole arena of life. And after having forgotten all of us and Baba suddenly the dawn of total wisdom will come upon you. No matter what the situation Baba's words will set you free to deal with it like a sage.' The exorcist leader's words were so powerful that I felt as if I was being pushed back physically, and my mind was in a daze.

'So you are all showing me precisely what you want to show me and nothing else?', I said somewhat heatedly.

'My dear friend', said the exorcist leader, 'Have something to eat and drink, and be free from apprehensions. In the time you have at your disposal, you can never understand generations of folklore and moreover you don't have anyone to help you gather data. So don't agitate! You are getting everything in a golden platter!' I did not know what to say to this speech except to feel a sudden and deep indifference. What the exorcist leader said was more than true and at the crux of my dilemma. I never really had believed I could study a whole region of the hill folks religion and ritual sitting in Devagiri and had already made some excursions to nearby villages. All to no avail, and my feeling of trying to empty the ocean with a spoon only grew in proportion to my desperate efforts at participant observation. Yet I consoled myself that my effort was sincere and that I could give at least a vignette of what prevailed in that region, and in Devagiri itself.

My plan for the day was to have a brief meeting with the Baba and after taking a brief repast I went down to his hut. It was quite spacious and Baba was sitting in front of a dhuni fire, having put a Grey shawl around his shoulders. I went in from the low door and sat down in front of him. He enquired after my food and staying arrangements and once he was satisfied about them he was clearly ready to answer my questions.

'Baba, last night in the lower temple I had the experience of burning on a funeral pyre. My entire body lit up with heat and I was in an undifferentiated state. At first I felt a bit uncomfortable but later it was a pleasant warmth. Can you tell me what this experience means. Can you tell me what a man feels on his funeral pyre. It is something that makes me feel very uneasy'.

'Contrary to what people believe there is a residual sensation left in the body when a man is cremated. What you experienced is what happens when a man is cremated. His whole body lights up with heat that is not uncomfortable and later it cools down. So there is no pain, nor is there any discomfort. Death takes the soul and he goes to the gates of the Death Keeper Yama.

Yama is very objective and sends the soul to whichever hell or heaven he is most suited for'. Baba smiled a bit.

'Do you mean to say that hell and heaven exist? Aren't they are figment of someone's imagination?' I was curious to see what he would say.

'Heaven (swarga) and Hell (naraka) are vibrational areas where the appropriate treatment is meted out to the souls that go there. The feeling that they are illusory is due to people trying to buy comfort at the cost of Truth. The various souls are weeded out and those who go to swarga have no possibility of complaining so wonderful is everything out there. Good men, men of learning, artists, philosophers, yogis, and in general those who have led a good moral life are eligible for Heaven. Those who have perpetuated mischief and been criminal in their attitudes and deeds are hurled into hell where there is nothing but problems of all sorts and enmity and hatred. This is something which is obvious to anyone who has progressed somewhat on the path of spirituality. Be sure of one thing, the after life is not in anyone's imagination it is even more real than the average man's perception of the world of matter.'

'So man should lead a good life otherwise he will have to undergo untold miseries after he dies-but what about before he dies? Many criminals and brigands and so on seem to be enjoying a good life!' I thought I had driven in a hard point.

'Such people are living a life of pleasure and this cannot go on for very long. In fact such people are most frightened and insecure at heart. Many of them turn a new leaf when they can no longer experience pleasure and their senses have become jaded. Even this is better than to try and whip up the senses with drugs and drink and try to go on blindly as before. There is nothing in your statement that cannot be easily refuted. The purpose of life is the conquest of the Self (atman) and it's dissolution into Brahman. That is the aim of life and anything that goes counter to it is folly of the highest degree'. Baba seemed pensive.

'Then there must be some method for doing all this?' I asked hopefully. Whenever the question of way or method had come up in my discussions with holy men they had started giving long lectures and describing impossible yogic practices.

'Well I know from the way you say it that this is your standard question and you ask it in a tone of sheer disappointment. My friend let me give you a gift. I will give you a way that will never fail you, although you may fail it. Inside every person on this earth there is a meter of sorts which tells a man what is right and what is wrong. The religions of the world are a witness to what I am saying. And man always knows whether what he is doing is right, or whether he is doing wrong. It is his accursed mind so full of ambition, greed competitiveness and ego that is the obstacle that prevents him from always following the good and the right path. People fall into the habit of listening to their mind which is always frightened and insecure rather than the way of the spirit which is beyond the intellect. They rationalize saying that if we do this good act we are bound to suffer in so many ways. Reasoning thus they ignore the indications given by the spirit. So be bold and do not fear while doing the good and the right. The warnings will come to you clearly and it requires only a clear sight and the will power, the guts, to do the right thing. If you can do only this much your position among the great men and women of the world past, present and future is assured. That is all they have done! All they have done is follow the voice of the spirit at any cost. And let me tell you the spirit is never unkind and never makes an unfair demand. It is only the mind of man that is confused and had centuries of imprinting. That imprinting can be set aside if we follow the murmuring of the Spirit'. There was a complete silence in my mind, and my eyes were brimming with tears. Baba had spoken so sincerely and with such simplicity that I felt that I had nothing more to ask him, not that morning at any rate.

'Can I go and follow those rituals of the exorcists?' I asked him.

'Do you mean to say you are already 'full'. Are you already satisfied?' Baba leaned forward and rubbed my head lightly.

'Go', he said 'Come back for more in the evening, and don't worry about what you ask me. You can satisfy your curiosity in any direction so far as I am concerned.' I touched his feet and left the hut in a daze. The sun had started peeking out and a bit of the ice ranges were visible. I felt as if I was ten feet tall. For the first time in my life I had obtained an answer to spiritual practice which completely satisfied me. I turned my mind to doing some research on the exorcists. I could hear them chanting in the higher temple.

I went through the day in a concentrated state of mind, and have recorded the rituals and their sociological meaning in my thesis. However the conversations that I had with Bhagavad Baba were noted down by me but I felt they had little to do with orthodox exorcism procedures. The ideas of the Baba were in a realm of their own and I still don't feel that they would shed light on the exorcists procedures for two reasons. The first is that the Baba did not participate in the exorcist proceedings; and the second is that the exorcists themselves did not have any intellectual questioning to do with the Baba simply because their schedule did not permit them to sit near the Baba and ask questions close to their heart.

That evening I went to the Baba when the sun was

going down and laid down some wild flowers that I had gathered for him. He was in a semi-trance and his eyes were half open and half shut. I did not have to be told that the Baba was best off on this isolated remote mountain spur. He had in fact sought out just such a spot from which he had to stir only once in a while, or not at all. I wondered aloud to him what would happen when the area was cordoned off from the Lower Plateau. Where would his food supplies come from, for instance? Baba was quite cool in his reply and left me flabbergasted.

'I have a lot of friends in the army and these young friends will not only keep me supplied with rations, they will go to the extent of keeping me in firewood also. The spring supplies me with water and in the winter I can light a fire and go into the lower temple and be quite warm. So don't worry about me, I am O.K.'

'I have been wondering in a subconscious way about what you said earlier this morning', I said. 'The area of confusion is what I began with namely the experience of death. While most of the world religions talk of a heaven of sorts, it is Sanatana Dharma alone which makes an issue of life after death. It is treated with absolute seriousness, and is not a passing statement or something which happens by the way. As such most world religions create an atmosphere of 'this is the only life', and advise to live it fully, by which it is presumed that pleasures should be pursued with dedication. I am interested in your knowledge of death and facts connected with it. I am afraid I may be repeating myself a little but without an understanding of this subject there would be no enlightenment, no security of emotions and no peace of mind'. I looked at Baba in a kind of beseeching desperation. This series of questions in my mind had never been answered textually or orally no matter whom I had asked about them.

'Young fellow', said Baba, 'Ask one question at a time. Be sure I will tell you whatever you want to know about Life , Death, Hereafter......anything!' Baba sounded amused, and I could detect a little smile hovering on his face. The fact that he was taking me seriously was a consolation and I planned to make full use of this unique opportunity of meeting an enlightened sage with whom I felt perfectly at ease and was not afraid of treading on his toes a bit, in order to come by near extinct wisdom.

'What happens when a person dies?' I had deliberately kept the question simple. I wanted to know the answer to this question which had perplexed even the Vedic sages who by the end of their queries were still groping for an answer. Baba who was the prototype of the Vedic sages who lived reclusively, I felt, might have an answer. I wanted to find out.

'Death means that the physical body we call 'me', 'myself' and 'I', breaks apart. It's functioning ceases, and the person breathes no longer, is not able to move, cannot see or think...........he is dead. When a person is no longer able to have any volition, cannot breathe and has no pulse, that person is dead. As regards the experience of dying that is a different matter. It is as if a slow paralysis sets up in the body as the spirit (atman) moves out of the body like a vapour, a sort of mist that is made of fine particles of gases and is really not homogenous. As this mist moves out of the pores of the body, it starts getting stiff and when the vapours have gone out the body becomes like a board of wood. Meanwhile as this happens the vapours start forming a body of vapour, bit by bit, until it coheres and is actually similar to the physical body that has died. But by no means are they identical ! This mistake should not be made. The vapour body to which the spirit has now shifted is meant to live in a world with much higher vibrations, and cannot be seen by the mourners. Yet if there is a gifted yogi or clairvoyant he would be able to sight the vapour body, and he would see that until the rites of death are not completely over the vapour body is not quite free to go where it pleases but is attached to the physical dead body like a kite on an anchor. Once the rites are over, rites which the vapour body has to attend and witness, the vapour body can move about in the other world merely by willing to move. The vapour body moves by thought and will, although it can walk if it wishes if it comes across some glorious landscape which some other vapour bodies have created in the other world'. Baba stopped there and made a gentle gesture indicating whether he should continue.

'Why does it take so long for the vapour body to be free of the physical?' I asked Bhagavad Baba.

'It takes quite long for the vapour body to form and the rituals have been made by seers to take account of this fact.The body should not be cremated straight after death, in a hurry. It should be allowed to release every bit of spirit vapours before it is cremated or put into samadhi. However if one looks at the length of time that the vapourous body is going to live, then it is obvious that it forms very quickly. The vapourous body lasts indefinitely and disintegrates only when its every wish is fulfilled. In fact it can correctly be said that the vapourous body is immortal, and dies only when it wants to. It cannot be killed by any known means except it's own volition, and this happens when it is ready to diffuse into Brahman, and gain Moksa, the Final Liberation. But my dear son Moksa is not a joke! It is truly the end of all individuality and the vapourous body if ready for it simply drops into the vibrations of Brahman like a drop of water into the sea. So after death usually the vapourous body pursues those areas of life which it was not able to while it was in the physical body, be it asceticism or hedonism!' Baba clapped his hands dramatically, making me jump a bit on my perch.

'Baba, please tell me more about the possibilities of doing things after one has gone into the vapour body. What exactly do you mean when you say the vapour body can pursue what it likes , be it a pursuit of pleasure, or a pursuit of spiritualism?' I was truly interested in knowing what one could do in the vapour body and what were the possibilities for action in the sphere of the other world where the spirits roamed and fulfilled their wishes.

'The vapour body is made of fine vapours of different types and is quite capable of feeling, sensing, thinking, moving and doing just about anything and everything that a physical body can. However the vapourous body feeds itself only on vibratory matter and therefore it is not possible for it to swallow physically anything, nor to carry anything material. In fact there is no waste matter in the vapour body and it is completely pure. This is well in keeping with the world of spirit which is completely pure in itself. The vapour body through it's power of mentation can build even cities, continents, worlds even universes through its creative efforts......... but naturally that bent of mind must exist. Great seers and holy people live in the other world in harmony with each other, running their schools and ashrams. If a vapour body wants it can join one of these spiritual schools. You see, time is not a problem in the world of vapourous vibrations, nor is there any need for cooking or eating food. So man is equal to his talent in any field and nothing else matters. Yes! Those spirits which have no interest in the imaginative and creative spiritual pursuits of the vapour world, very soon will themselves into one or other of the worlds where there is a possibility of simulating completely any type of pleasure, simple or complex and enter into that vibratory space. There they play out their fantasies which are far more real than in the material world, and then go into hibernation until a suitable animal or human womb is found to bring them back into a material world. So the world of vapourous, or gaseous vibrations is one where everything that is desired in the material world is available, and the only method of realizing them is the limits of the imagination. You may think that one could live forever pursuing the pleasures of the senses but a time comes, sooner rather than later that the vapour body is fed up with sensations and seeks to purify itself. To do that however it must go into a material womb once again, and don't doubt it, many of the hedonists go down into animal wombs suitable to their desire for purgating themselves from the burden of sensations. On the other hand there are the great schools and ashrams where gargantuan experiments are being made for the upliftment of the spirit in all material worlds not simply the earth!' Baba stopped and sipped some tea that one of the exorcists had brought us. As for me I was reeling under the onslaught of new concepts and ideas which I had no doubt half thought or half imagined but never in this clear way. Suddenly my life started seeming to be a little more precious and my time on earth something that had to be made the best of. I was shivering despite the fire burning in the middle of the room.Baba passed me a blanket as my teeth had started chatterring and I could hardly articulate my sentences without sounding most confused. I drank the hot tea in silence and my mind was blank. I had somewhere in my imagination already made up mind that my questions would be evaded or only half answered. Baba had in fact put me into a dilemma : the limits to my life were not time or money but my will and creative imagination, brought together under the umbrella of my spiritual journey. I was suddenly caught in the grip of a fear that constricted my throat, and the thought occurred to me with tremendous velocity that were not the exorcists and the

Baba really beautiful and good human beings, I should be worried for my life. I had heard of people from the plains coming to the hills and getting lost, never to be found again. Being with Baba and looking at his kind shining brown eyes dispelled my paranoia, which to my mind was not an exaggerated imagination at all.

I tried to make conversation with Baba but despite the tea I seemed to have lost control over my speech and even more determined effort I ended up biting my tongue painfully. Baba gestured for me to go to sleep, and I left the hut after giving back the blanket. I made a final effort to speak with the exorcist leader asking him about the day and areas that I was not able to observe and found to my surprise that my voice was back and I had gained control of my tongue again. I surmised that Baba did not want to talk further that night and had done something to me. I was sure he was quite capable of it, what with the endless years of yogic practices.

This night and the subsequent nights I slept in a corner of the lower temple and not very close to the fire. One experience of virtually being 'cremated' was enough to keep me from feeling ungrateful so far as the lack of proximity from the log fire was concerned. From the third night onward till we left the Higher Plateau I slept in a corner of Baba's hut after he had inspected it carefully and made sure that scorpions, snakes, and other insects with nasty stings were not lurking in the place where I was to sleep.

The weather had turned glorious on the eve of the second day there and the magnificent snows of the mountains enthralled us. From Devagiri the snows looked as if they were directly in front of us but from the spur on the Higher Plateau they looked as if they were a little below us. Some of the mountains however were such that it seemed we could literally stretch our hands out and touch them. It was an awe inspiring sight, and in retrospect I feel it was as if one had truly reached the climax of one's perceptual life. The snows stretched out against the deep blue sky, with a few wisps of clouds stretched out lazily over the peaks was a sight that beggarred any description of Heaven. I felt truly that if there was a Heaven anywhere then I was in it.

Little wonder then that despite the cold winds and the spartan rations we were all enthused with the work we had on hand. The rituals went on all day, full of fervour and devotion and I would join in unobtrusively for as long as I could participate. However as soon as I had got the gist of the rites, and felt I could pick up the rest of the strands later I would make a bee line for the hut of Bhagavad Baba. By the time I used to get to his hut it was midday and he would be busy with tidying his hut, sunning his straw mattress and cooking his meager meal. He never missed making tea for the two of us, but would refuse to talk anything about his views and experiences in spirituality. Whenever I tried to get him involved in any such conversation he would say that I should wait till the evening. According to him I was undergoing a metamorphosis which would unfold all throughout my life and during the day I should let the silence of mind that had crept in on me there to expand and deepen further. It was from that silence that the conversation we had in the late evening, would make sense and benefit me the most. I found that I could get myself a perch on the spur and gaze at the mighty snows and observe how suddenly and quickly that the great mountains changed their moods, and mine with them. I had never been so enthralled in all my life and I felt a sensation of utter gratitude to nature, and to my fate for having brought me to the Higher Plateau. In that feeling of sheer bliss I lost my appetite for food and drank only water and tea, apart from a few morsels of food that Baba gave me on a leaf.

Thus my routine for those few days in the Higher

Plateau gave me an opportunity to gaze the splendid snow mountains to my hearts content and the weather held in the daytime. Towards the late evening it would sometimes get clouded over but the mists would clear by midmorning the next day. In fact after the second day the perception of time that I had blended so absolutely that I do not know to this day how much time we spent on the Higher Plateau. I could have lived there forever, or dropped dead with an exhaustion I did not feel. As time passed my body became extremely sensitive and I felt light as a feather to the extent that I had to logically remind myself that I was flesh and blood.

Thus the conversations with Baba became for me a long continuity of questions and answers without specific dates attached to them. However surprisingly enough I went through my participant observation and questions to Baba without any serious disorientation. However I do remember that the questions I asked Baba were fundamental ones because I still remember the main flow of our exchanges. On the second evening, just before this strange amnesia beset me I talked to Baba a little more about Death and the Beyond. I sat in front of him while he squatted on his straw mattress, covering his bare shoulders with a thin blanket. He was silent but I could sense that I should commence the interaction.

'Baba I have observed many times that the dead person looks so entirely devoid of life that obviously something has left the body and it is the end. Does anything survive? I know I have raised this question differently to you earlier but my thirst for knowing it from you is not at all quenched!' I waited for his input keenly.

'I once went to a cremation ground and saw the body of a young man lying motionless on the cremation platform. They had not yet covered his face and from a distance it looked as if someone was sleeping. I went closer and saw that he was already stretched out on the wood of the pyre below. He was a young barber and his friends told me that he was about twenty five years of age and had died of a heart attack.

'On the pyre next to him was the body of a man who I had come to cremate and he was eighty years and more. When his face was uncovered for the rites his face looked dark and devoid of any life. He was obviously no more.

'Now one man died at twenty five and the other lived over eighty. What is the difference between the two. Was the man who lived up to a ripe old age more fortunate than the one who died young?' Bāba stopped and raised his hand for my comment.

'I have no idea what you are talking about. If I am to speak about the death of the two men I would say that both had finished their journey on earth and therefore had to depart. What I am asking however is that did anything survive their respective deaths, or not?' I was treading very warily.

'You see, a lot has to do with what you believe, and that is why religion and spirituality are so important. What happens after death is what you firmly believe all your life, not as something which is thrust upon you, but what you have pondered. If the young man had any chance of pondering life and death his beliefs would have materialized. But I doubt that very much.At such a young age life is just beginning and there is little time to evaluate matters which are of ultimate significance. Similarly in the case of the aged man who died it would all depend on his belief patterns. If he truly believed in the hereafter he would on death enter the hereafter. If he believed that life ends with the body his life force would simply diffuse and go back to the elements. So you see what happens after death is what we actually believe is going to happen... but not too many people have solid well thought out beliefs and that is why in the Sanatana Dharma the importance of the guru is paramount. The guru says believe in me and I will show you eternal life. Of course it is much easier to travel the spiritual journey alongside the guru, rather than build your own raft or ship. And many people have put their faith in such spiritual masters over the ages and in fact this is the tradition in Sanatana Dharma. Yet regarding the two men I was referring to it was obvious that the young man had no idea regarding the hereafter or had ever thought about it; and the aged man was obviously confused and had come to no proper belief about it. I would say that both died ignorant and their spirit simply dissipated into the elements. They were truly no more. There was no body, no belief, no name, no heaven or hell. It was a case of eternal deep, dreamless sleep. They had gone into the void and dissolved in it' Baba stopped and readjusted his blanket about his bony frame and asked me to get him a glass of water.

'This is rather devastating', I said. 'It seems to imply that a huge majority of people will get some type of Black Nirvana when they die for most of us have no firm or solid belief regarding the hereafter. Is this the position so far as any religion is concerned, or this is the situation with Hindus alone?' I was getting a bit agitated as my pet ideas were being battered.

'The point that you are missing is that life beyond death takes place in a vapourous body made of compounded gases. This body can sense and perceive. However for this body to form there has to be a firm will in it's existence during the life of a person. If that belief is there then on death the body will form and the ancestors or the guru will take possession and care of the vapour bady. But what can anybody do if the vapour body doesn't form? One can only watch in dismay as the gases and vapour blow away like smoke and the person is completely erased. That is the reason that all manner of meditation is recommended, and that is the reason why the guru and the company of believers (satsangha) is recommended because together they can, and do make an entire world where they stay and continue their spiritual practices, so that they can remain alive forever in world after world of their collective creation!' Baba made a gesture as if to say that what he was saying was obvious.

'That means that life exists after Death. That it is possible for awareness and consciousness of a person to survive forever?'

'Under given circumstances, it is possible for consciousness and perception and awareness to exist forever. Even the name of a person can survive forever but to do so the person would naturally have had something great and good in him during his lifetime which he developed with great care. But then a man survives even if he is of a grossly material type provided he has built up his concentration in that direction. But it certainly won't be in a heaven where there is satsangha. It will be a Hell where each denizen is out to cut his throat, cheat and lie to him. But, yes, such people who love material things passionately also survive. In fact it is the passionate people who survive in one or the other of the many worlds that exist. However those without passion, no interest in life except to gripe and groan, well such people go into the trash can, and become manure for nature's forces'. It was clear that one aspect of the discussion was over. I too had little interest left in the theory of the subject and Baba had come across neatly. I had realized what had always been embedded in my deeper consciousness, that it is the collective spirit of man that is quite capable of creating a world of consciousness and to populate it with appropriate vapourous bodies and to live together in happiness for eternity, going from one world to another in an unbroken chain. This was a chain of worlds that already existed and religion was an ingress into these worlds. The religious man and the spiritual man were thus not losing sight of the future and working for it right now. It was a great solace for to have found a logical explanation for the fact that religion was factual and real and truly eased the aches and pains of the people who adhered to their religion. As a religious person myself I felt that fortunately I had invested much time in areas which would be of use to me not only in the 'here', but also in the 'hereafter'.

The exorcist rituals occupied my mind in different ways now. One of these perspectives was that of the anthropologist; the other of a person genuinely interested in eternal religion. As I watched the rituals of devotion, the rituals in which sacred songs were sung, and the sacred dances around the sacred fire in the higher temple where the bust of the deities was displayed under a small cover I realized that the exorcists were weaving together a fabric for the villagers. The believers would benefit from that texture and fabric even after their lives. The village as I saw it was a religious community which perpetuated its reality in the hereafter through these rituals.

In fact it struck me that the rituals of exorcism, ranging from the brief ones that lasted about half an hour to these elaborate ones were part of the foundation of the world to come. The solidarity of the village was not just an economic one but a religious entity in itself. Many facts of the Indian village have changed over the years, and especially over the last fifty years, but the fact of the religious oneness of the village is intact. The exorcists made it clear to me that they were bound together in a spiritual bond that had an indefinite beginning, and no end. They would meet in life after life in this or other worlds, until they were totally cleansed of all spiritual and sensory impurities, and were ready to go into the oblivion of Brahman. The leader was especially categorical about this.

'When, sir, you ask what is the purpose of these rituals, we always tell you it is for the good of Devagiri. You say you understand, and we keep silent. But here in this most sacred of our temples I have to inform you that this is not restricted to good crops, and good health. It is also important for the good friendship between people within the village and our relations with other villages surrounding us. And above all these rituals relate to our strengthening the base of our spiritual abode which is none other than the spiritual Devagiri which is populated by different deities and where Siva and Kali live during our festive celebrations. Yes, we maintain and further create village Devagiri among the heavens. This is the reason our youth is willing to risk their lives coming up to the Higher Plateau every two years and go through rigorous hardships in the village exorcisms every year. It is not because of blind religious fervor or some blind reason. We know that we will all meet again and we have to make preparations for these meetings. These rituals are directed at our spiritual Devagiri even more than our concern for better crops, good health among the villagers and their livestock. For us the outcome of this ritual in the wilderness is more important to us than our physical bodies. Now do you understand?' The exorcist leader a man in his early thirties was quite emphatic about what he said. I did not have to reply at length but told him that it was very kind of him to have made a point that could be misunderstood. Further what the young exorcist leader had said made sense to me as a spiritually oriented man, and I was sure that what the exorcists were saying through their spiritual fervors and their spiritual actions went far beyond mere anthropology. It had to do with the domain that anthropology could only hope to record but not to enter. To enter into the world of the exorcists a man would have to leave behind him all his baggage of theories and data and dissolve into the beliefs that they had developed over the immeasurable ages . These beliefs of the village being a religious and spiritual whole which could not be split, were beliefs that had come down from the depths of the eternal religion and were not the monopoly of any age, or place. They truly belonged to humanity and any individual who would like to be part of them. It was clear to me that the world of the vapourous selves was not a lonely chaotic world, but had been planned and put together during the spiritually dedicated lifetime of the villagers. A villager dying had no fear of death and was quite sure that he would find himself in Devagiri again after death. The only difference would be that the Devagiri he woke up in was a spiritual Devagiri and there he would be welcomed by his friends and relatives and start to work for the upkeep and upliftment of his co brothers and sisters. It was only too obvious that the good cheer of the villagers, their stupendous generosity and their god fearing nature stemmed entirely in their absolute certainty that whatever a person did he was accountable for. Evil could never come in the way of good, and there was no escape from one's deeds whether they were good or bad. That evening I put a related question to Bhagavad Baba who now that the ice was broken was quite affable with me and had even offered to let me sleep in a corner of his hut which I had politely declined. I knew that a holy man values his privacy more than anything else. Moreover since the last few months I had developed a habit of snoring at periodic intervals and did not want to burden him with my presence. Baba was however insistent and told me that he did not mean that I should necessarily go to sleep but that I could talk to him uninterrupted and also to do some uninterrupted meditation.

'In this marvellous mountaintop, it would be really nice if you could spend a few nights meditating and talking about spirituality. Otherwise your coming all this way would have definitely gone waste. In fact from now on till the time you leave let the exorcists do their chanting and singing at night alone. You come to my hut and pursue your own discipline. You will see how much strength there is in this little known mountain spur. Don't worry so much about your work at night. During the day you can be with the exorcists but leave off at about midday and prepare yourself for the night. You will find that this spur is fantastic to get in touch with your favourite deity. The images would be very clear and I can already see that you are restless to be in direct contact with your Ista Devi. So don't lose this opportunity'

When Bhagavad Baba made his point I realized with a sense of deep depression that all the activity had kept me from contemplating and talking to Maha Maya despite all the promises I had made to myself. In fact I had almost dropped my meditative practices in the midst of all the hubbub around the work I had to do. My depression mysteriously turned to elation as I realized that I could use the dhuni fire in Baba's hut to gaze and get in touch with Maya, if she wasn't too cross with me for my sheer laziness in getting in contact with her. I made sure that evening that I had a cold water bath near the spring and put on my spare shirt which was relatively clean. The weather had held out and the wind had not been too harsh, and I was full of anticipation about what Maya would tell me. It was indeed a unique opportunity to get in touch with her, if I could.

Bhagavad Baba had laid out some straw for me in one corner of his hut and I tended the fire while he had gone down to the spring. I had been shivering incessantly from the cold and the night set in very early, yet the view of the late evening sun on the ice peaks was unearthly in its beauty. I did some stretching and bending exercises to warm myself up. When Baba returned he saw that I was still shivering and made me a herbal potion which I sipped and a pleasant warmth went through my body. I felt that I was tingling all over. Baba and I talked in monosyllables when we did talk. It was clear to me that we would be meditating together, each going into our own world and both coming back recharged with our experiences. I did not feel like eating but Baba had made some unleavened bread which we had with some cooked lentil and hot tea. Baba told me that we would have a break after the midnight hour which would be signalled by the exorcists ringing the bell by the icons at the higher temple. They would be celebrating the half way point of their rites and rituals and Baba assured me that the sound of the bells would reach Devagiri three thousand feet below. I was incredulous and felt that this seemed a rather difficult proposition but then I had learned that what does not seem possible is often very simple for the people concerned.

I settled myself comfortably in the straw mattress and put the jute sack over it. I wrapped a shawl that I had brought with me around my shoulders and went into a mantra meditation, chanting silently within the mind. I wanted to calm myself down from the excitement all around before I attempted to gaze into the sacred fire and touch up with Maya. I felt terribly anticipative about what was going to happen. A lot of water had gone under the bridge since the last time I had gazed upon Maya and I had a tight knot in my belly wondering what she would say about my performance. I had always been interested about her opinion about my work in the world and was therefore very nervous. The mantra meditation calmed me down considerably and I heard a voice within me say 'Don't worry, everything will be alright', and this repeated itself a number of times and I felt the time was ripe to shift to gazing the sacred fire.

At first nothing seemed to happen, and I began to fear that my attempt would end in disaster. It was crucial that Maya let me have her darshan in this holy spur, otherwise I would read it as something which would be catastrophic for me. I began to get very depressed and unhappy and even began to weep and sob silently and then suddenly I saw her! She was sitting below a large oak tree leaning against it's trunk. She wore a turquoise coloured sari dress and her long black hair was loosely hanging around her face haloing it with a sort of cascade, that looked like a dark waterfall of thick honey. She was smiling radiantly and I immediately cottoned on to the major difference in her presence this time – she looked like a mother. There was something radiant about her and she had a look of fulfillment. For a long moment I just gazed upon her taking in her spiritual beauty. I was sure once again that I had never seen such an alluring woman in my entire life. She was literally oozing beauty and charm, apart from having an incredible aura of grace around her. I was sure that she had kept herself aloof from the women of the earth simply because beside her the best of them would have looked quite ordinary. The whole atmosphere around her was that of utter spiritual power and beauty. In my mind I bowed down to her and genuflected at her feet. She was quite relaxed and behaved as if the whole thing did not matter at all, and that these formalities should not be encouraged. But how else would I make contact with her lotus feet and come in touch with her spiritual self. As soon as I touched her I saw myself sitting a few feet in front of her and despite the chronological time being early evening Maya's time was a sunny afternoon. She seemed to be in a good mood and thinking of someone or something. Wave after wave of misty smiles went lightly over her fair face like ripples of water in a translucent lake. I understood how millions of men and women had agreed to do whatever she asked of them even in their dreams. I understood that there was no way beyond Maya unless she herself willed it to be so, for she was the ultimate vision, a vision that commanded everything that a person could possess.

I began to think that this was going to be basically darshan and that was enough for me. Gradually Maya seemed to enter back into the scenery around us. We were on a hillside close to the spur and there was no one on the spur. The plumes of smoke that were emanating from the lower and higher temples as the sacred fires were lit looked incredibly feminine and poetic. Though it certainly looked as part of the spur, and I could see the snows in the brilliant sunlight, nevertheless there was no one there with us. I dared not talk unless Maya addressed me. It would have been sacrilege to so because she seemed to be in an especially mercurial mood, and I did not want to take the risk of disturbing her. Then suddenly her eyes were locked with mine and I felt a blaze of fire go through my belly. If I hadn't already been sitting I would have fallen down so intense was the pain in the pit of my belly, at the sternum.

'That is for forgetting all about me after you left Sri Turiya, and went back for your work. But I understand please don't tell me that one more time. Don't worry I can see that you have not found someone else to follow, but that it's just a matter of not having had the right atmosphere to meditate upon me. I know you have thought about me a lot and that you realize that I have been taking you forward by the nose. No you have not abandoned me, and I have not and will not abandon you.

In fact in this last period your love for me has become one which a child has for his mother and that is why I am so distracted. The last time you gazed upon me you were like a romantic lover. Well it's alright and this would keep on changing from time to time. You need protection in what you are doing, building a house in Devagiri and I advise you that from now on till your time in Devagiri is over you should make it a point to keep constantly in touch with me inwardly so that I can tell you what you should do to build a nice house and to do your other work too. The people here are nice but the situation has to be kept track of because you don't have much time to put together your house and even less time to put together your research. Yes, it was I who ensured that you get to the Higher Plateau, otherwise the very basis for your study on the exorcists would be impossible. Do you realize that the ritual that you are tracking and noting takes place once in two years and that the cordoning off of the Higher Plateau is going to change the whole face of ritual in this area as one of the most exotic locales for prayer meditation and devotion is going to grow desolate again. You will never meet Baba again after these few days and this seems to be the pattern of your life. Many of the people who have had an impact on your life seem to have met you only briefly. Anyway I have come into your life to stay. After countless lifetimes and countless disappointments you have come to me with all that you have in terms of love, affection, and faith, and let me tell you I will not let you down, I will not play games and make impossible demands, and above all I will not play you off with some other and leave you hanging on the verge of despair.'

Maya had paused for a while but I could not help feeling that she had the pulse of my situation. Every woman that I had desired to get close to had begun the game of playing me off against other people to the point that I had to withdraw out of self respect. This had led ultimately to a situation that I had become very wary of women and kept to myself and a few good friends. In fact this type of practice of encouraging me seemed to be endemic to my proposed lady friends. As soon as I thought that I was getting closer to friendship and psychological intimacy I would be gradually shown my place and several alternatives would be paraded in front of me. This would both be irritating and painful and I had ended up being a person with few friends and many acquaintances. Maya was right. I had perhaps kept from meditating and gazing upon her for fear that the endless pattern would repeat. That would be really heartbreaking for me. Maya meant more to me than my life, rather she was my life.

'I was afraid that perhaps you would disappear from my life, because most women who had started coming closer to me somehow changed their mind about our relationship and disappeared really fast failing to even keep up a face saving relationship. Maybe I mistook this pattern was going to repeat.' I was rather apologetic for what was clearly cowardly behaviour.

'You don't have to worry anymore about all that. Usually when a person is reaching out in a big way towards the inner self many difficulties begin to appear before him. This could be a craze for a drug, women, wealth, fame... it could be anything that comes in the way. For you it was the repeated disappointments in the experience of love. You see, nobody's perfect and a romantically inclined person such as you tends to fantasize that your women friends are perfect. Naturally this is a terrifying context to live up to. They back off not because they don't like you but because it would be very difficult to live up to your expectations of them. Then of course you come and stand in front of me and see me in your gazing. Gradually you start going berserk and see me not just in your gazing but also in your day to day perception you mistake women for me. You are convinced that you are well on your way to total derangement, which is true in a way. So, naturally you stop gazing and looking for me because your obsession is now turning into a neurosis that will derail you totally. Your fear of me turns you into an amusing fellow and I feel that I am being sought out seriously... do you understand?' Maya was looking so hypnotically beautiful that I had difficulty in tearing my eyes away from her eyes and looking at the snows beyond. As was usual in my encounters with her time stood still.

'Is there something wrong to fall in love,.even if it is at the drop of a hat?' I wanted to hear what she said about this.

'There is nothing wrong to fall in love, at all. But then let us be realistic, and not expect the person we love to suddenly turn around and reciprocate our feelings. How do they know that they are not being taken for a ride and that the 'love' that is being professed is not just a physical attraction? So to love is natural and to feel that this love is not quite right is also natural. This is one of the greatest battles of the spirit. Reciprocal love is usually a fantastic dream, and even when someone feels that it has happened the whole edifice collapses within a few months or years but it is all consuming while it lasts. So this is a spiritual test. The way to overcome disappointment in love is not to expect very much in return, apart from an acknowledgement which itself is likely to be oblique. When a man realizes that the all important thing is to love, and finds his satisfaction in loving then he is usually already past the need for physical passion. In any case physical passion will remain an obsession with mankind no matter what anyone says. I have arranged it that way and it's important that the fiery feeling of birthing a new generation remain as one of the several outstanding experiences in being a human. To love spiritually however is a different matter altogether. Once this is attained over lifetimes of effort we can say that the road is now wide open to enter into different worlds where spiritual love is not the monopoly of a few advanced sojourners but the basic nature of all the denizens of that world.'

'Am I going to get to this point or is this life of mine going to go round in circles till it drives me to despair?' I asked.

'You will be okay in your middle age, but before that you are destined for a lot of bumps, a ride which is rough. But you'll pull through. Yes, you'll realize that even Maya has a deep recess of incandescent spirituality.' Maya giggled like a mountain stream, soon breaking out into laughter that rippled like a cool mountain breeze. I blushed at the insinuations in her laughter and dared not to get into discussion. As it is my gazing would sometimes make the images a bit wobbly and it would appear that I was looking into a pond with her image in it being shaken by ripples of a pebble.It started getting out of focus and then became crystal clear. I knew that Maya was not going to come again that evening but also knew that she would never leave in a huff. She was much more beautiful than any woman I had ever seen but at the same time she had very limited frills. She seldom threw tantrums except to frighten or entertain her devotees. I asked her about my house and my research in Devagiri.

'You will manage alright, but beware you have little time with the Kaptan, and be sure you play it straight. You will be able to gather your data and to more or less finish the house. Put your concentration on that now when you get back and on the exorcist rituals here while you are here. Bhagavad Baba is a kind soul and has some idea about reality, but remember that he has been in touch with the world in a very peripheral way. Yes, he is a hidden master, but then the kind of hiding we do is what makes us relevant, and to what extent. So make the rest of your stay in Devagiri relevant to the building of the house and the unearthing of data. It will take years before you will be able to have the feel of freedom and love again in this fantabulous manner so let these feelings sink in. Then wind up your affairs in Devagiri and go back and finish your work. Gazing for me could only be counterproductive as I am going off the line until you find that one day you are thinking of me again and that I am coming more into your gazing than just to remind you that I exist. You must understand that gazing on me these years which intervene between the 'now' and the 'then' would only slow down your progress and would lead to a huge waste of time. I promise I'll be back with you the moment you can love me and not expect anything in return. That's when you will be ready to gaze again at me and I will take charge again, this time for good. I hope you get the message?'

I did get the message and felt that what she was saying was right. I was a young man and had a long way to go before I could remotely call myself a man of the world. Naturally there was a sense of depression as she disappeared from vision and only the oak tree and the snows were visible but the deep imprint that she had left in me was to last me for all the long intervening years, and I had only to close my eyes to hear her rippling laughter and gushing voice. I did not reply as she had already gone. With the characteristic feeling that one was falling I found myself back in my body in Baba's hut. I got up as Baba was already moving about in preparation of another cup of tea before the early morning meditation. I had been with Maya since I began to gaze and it had felt like half an hour. Baba smiled at me.

'It is clear that you met her and she has told you to

pursue your path. Well that's what I told you myself. Finish building that house, which you fancy to be a sort of temple... and get enough material for your book. That will be the end of your journey so far as this area is concerned – so enjoy it.'

That morning I gazed into the sacred fire and saw views of the house being built. I had told the villagers that it would sort of a temple where they could come and discuss anything that they liked. I felt a wave of impatience go through me in Baba's hut. I went softly out of the hut into the early morning. The suns rays had just touched the top of the highest of the sacred snow mountains and it glowed like soft embers. The exorcists were up and about and going about their various chores. The next two days the goats were going to be sacrificed and offered to the deities, before being cooked and eaten as sanctified food. Throughout the day I watched the ceremonies carefully and made my notes, both in my mind and on paper. The next two days went by in a whirl of observing the rituals and talking with Baba, and the time at the Higher Plateau ended before we could properly settle down. The night before we left I had one last meeting with Baba at his hut.I was in serious need of advice as to how to get on with Kaptan who had of late started asking for money, as a loan. A loan I was sure that I would not get back. I had discovered he was very fond of drinking a local brew and in fact that seemed to be his preoccupation. I had resigned myself to this habit of his and we were friends nevertheless. Yet I was keen for Baba's input on my situation since I knew without the help and intervention of Kaptan Saab the building of the house was not going to be easy as he carried a lot of clout among the locals. Indeed despite his frail frame and age the locals dreaded to be on the wrong side of Kaptan Saab. I apprised Baba of the situation not omitting any of my hopes, aspirations, fears and possible strategies.

'You need not worry too much about this situation. What you have to be is very careful since drink makes a man very cunning and desperate, once he is hooked to it. Keep him on a tight lease and exercise tolerance and forbearance. Above all don't give up your meditation because you will get the strategy step by step when you meditate. You are absolutely right that if you have no time to build your house and must get it done in a hurry you will have to pay for it to Kaptan Saab or anyone else.'

'Am I doing the right thing? I mean the house is bang in front of the sacred snows a place fit to build a temple. And I am going ahead with all the manoeuvres that are required to get the work done.! I had sometimes felt pathetic due to the rules of the ground situation making me go against my will. Everywhere something needed to be done and this required at every turn some kind of placation.'

'You are not the only person in this area who has had to get his work done and pay his way through it. Wake up ! Realize that this is not an ideal world and to try to live by ideals alone will not fill your belly nor anyone else's. Yes do not get trapped by your helpers or adversaries in the village and play your moves close to the chest. You will lose a bit of money but my experience tells me that you will get your work done and doing so will give you great satisfaction. Try to see if you can get information from your workers and put it together into your book. From now on till you leave the hills it should now only be the building of the house and your meditation. The information will come of its own and you have already got a large amount of it. If you do not meditate then you will not be able to direct the flow of events nor make out what should or should not be done. This would be disastrous. As such when you go down you should be a changed man, but in a subtle way.

Do not let anybody know what you think and let them feel that your obsession with the house and the research data is all that you have in your mind'. I was back in the hut. Maya had gone like a mist, Baba got up and started tending the sacred fire and doing other related chores like breaking some wood for keeping the fire smoldering during the night.

I went to my corner and meditated on the mantra that Sri Turiya had given me feeling a sense of being isolated and surrounded by circumstances beyond my control. There was no one in the area that I could genuinely communicate with and it was then, high up on the mountain spur that it came to me that I would in all likelihood not be able to stay in the house I was building for much time, if at all.

The next morning was gloriously clear and we set back to the Lower Plateau and this time the paths were not slippery as before and it was much easier to get across the Death Rock, as I would like to call it. I still had a nauseating moment when I climbed up the foot and handholds and reached the plateau on top. From then on it was a matter of being connected again to the social world and it was a wonderfully elating feeling. I had never realized that I was so connected with society. After several hours of walking downhill we reached the temple at the Lower Plateau where we were greeted quietly by the priest who offered us some tea. We all sat together in a circle and meditated a while thanking the powers that be that we were back safe and sound. The priest decided that he would accompany us back to Devagiri and accompany the sacred ashes that the exorcists were carrying with them in a cloth bag. These were to be deposited at the exorcist temple in the village and mixed with the ashes of the exorcism that took place there every year. These ashes were used by the exorcists to heal various types of afflictions. It took us another four hours of walking before we reached the village with concrete structures held together with tarmacadum. The stark contrast of the structures that used slate as roofing and stones as the walls was quite stunning. Even in those days (the late seventies and early eighties of the last century) it was slowly becoming apparent that aesthetics and centuries old wisdom was giving way to convenience and economy. I was only too glad that we had gone through that village which seemed to have no one doing anything in the fields that evening. On reaching Devagiri we were greeted by the villagers and the priest from the lower temple put ashes on the foreheads of those who were present to greet us. There was a village feast that night in which there was pukka food, fried in oil. The males ate first along with the children and the rest of the people carried off their share to be eaten at home. I was dog tired and went back to my hut. I did not want to meet anyone and was lucky that no one in that part of the village was looking for me. The lamp in Kaptan Saab, house was off and I guessed that he had turned in early. I felt that after a good nights sleep in my hut and some meditation I would be okay to meet him. I had a dream that night that I was playing with Maya and that like in a typical Hindi movie script I was running around the trees teasing her and she was laughing. I woke up in the morning and remembered my dream and laughed out loud, but not for long. There was a knock on the door and I could hear Kaptan Saab's voice. I rolled over on the cot and went and opened the door. At that time early in the morning Kaptan seemed to be quite normal. He wanted a small loan and I gave it to him after telling him that I hardly had any money to spare. I asked him when the foundation for the house was going to be laid, and he told me that he had got the map passed and we owed someone some money. I was getting used to this though it never failed to annoy and disgust me, and I told Kaptan that I would give it in a day or two. He seemed satisfied with that.

'Okay, we will meet later in the day, after you are ready', said Kaptan Saab.

'Sure thing, Kaptan Saab', I said affectionately to him.

I realize that I am adumbrating a hidden master of a very different sort. A portrait of a man who used to drink every day of his waking life, and was virtually dead without the intake of the fiery liquid. In fact the mission of his life when awake and straight was to go hunting for prospective patrons who would support his lifestyle of drinking and eating food that he cooked himself. Rarely he had someone as his guest. One evening in Devagiri when negotiations for the land were going on Kaptan Saab invited me to dinner in his house. I told him that I didn't eat meat but would come nevertheless. A bottle of unopened rum stood on the small work table in front of us. I wasn't much of a drinker and I told him so. He was not worried and suggested I take it as a medicine. I took down the rum with water and soon began to feel the effect.

At that time also there was a moment of truth. It was not easy to live as Kaptan Saab was living literally day to day, right down to his finances. He was independent from the rest of his extended family that had links with soldiers working in the army. But Kaptan Saab depended on no single source of income and tried to raise his money each day by goodwill, wheedling, even issuing mild threats. Whatever the method the patron eventually parted with the money which was not much even in those days.

'Kaptan Saab', I said to him one day, by way of investigation, 'How come a man of your experience and stature drinks whenever he gets the opportunity. Isn't it something that you should be avoiding, especially at your age?' I said all this after I had had two or three stiff one's of rum and could work up an interest in the subject and felt a streak of decency in Kaptan Saab, which made him unusual.

'I was in charge of the liquor stocks in the Azad Hindi Army and I saw to it that everyone got his liquor. It was only at the end of that that I felt free to take my drink. I never wanted to go higher than the rank of Captain because I knew the war would be over soon and the only interest I had in the war was to do my best in combat. We however were given in charge of rations and the movements of rations so that the question of actually shooting and killing somebody hardly arose. On the other hand we had a lot of power in our hands. If I wanted I could freeze the liquor for my superiors and make them deeply frustrated. In fact there were so many ways of doing so that I thought that the rank of Captain was the best if one wanted to enjoy the army life.

'So I thought that in a system where liquor is a key to every door, why not hold the keys and play with the smart boys.Why not make them realize they were nothing without liquor. And then later when I left the army, after it had disbanded I came to the amazing conclusion that the whole of the society was in some way or the other trapped in putting life together through some drug or the other. I reached the conclusion that life goes round on the wheels of drugs, and mind you these drugs can be an innocuous dependence on heavy doses of tea, coffee, chewing tobacco, smoking tobacco, smoking cannabis related drugs, drinking alcohol and the abuse of allopathic drugs. Drugs which are immediately contraband are the opiates which ruin life rather than make it go round. Though I did try opium in my army days I found that it had extremely addictive qualities. I had been warned that within seven hits, each a matchhead in size spread over seven days I would be a hopeless opium addict, enslaved to the charms of the drug forever'.

'What is so attractive about it?' I asked Kaptan Saab.

'It is like a very attractive woman whose fatal flaw is that she has no character. Anyone who comes to her is given immense pleasure and respect, something that he can't find in the world at any cost, unless he is a conquering general. The price of opium is very low and many of the soldiers settled for the opium rush straight away. Just like I knew I could not pay the price that Madam O demanded, some of the others knew that that was exactly what they wanted.'

'Do you mean, that there is some sort of ejaculatory pleasure or is it something like the taste of good food?' I asked.

'It is as if the whole body has become a source of pleasurable sensations, and the perceptions have become very gentle though scintillating. Immediately the thought comes to the mind 'This is the best trip', and unless one takes recourse to the information that one has been given about it's power of enslavement, one would be well on one's way to be a beloved slave of the Grand Lady. That's what we used to refer to Opium in our days — the Grand Lady, The Big Madam, and Conquest of Love. We all knew that only a Monarch in the real sense of the term could use Big O without a hitch because he would get it regularly as a diet — while the rest of us are made to root and ferret for it and are made to feel demeaned and sick before we can get our regular dosage' Kaptan Saab poured out some rum for himself.

'What is it like relative to marijuana and hashish?' I asked.

'Well whatever the drawbacks of marijuana and hashish one doesn't die of taking too much, you just puke out, and have a rotten day or night, depending on when it is taken. Further there is a crucial difference. Opium adopts you immediately and clings you to her bosom, as if you were a lost child. On the other hand cannabis, bhang, marijuana, hashish, charas coming from the same plant picks you up and shakes you until you think you are going to go insane. Such strange and peculiar thoughts come into the brain that it is quite incapable of remaining quite the same. As such the Sanatanis have reserved a single day to experience this loss of ego. This is the most arduous path and requires intelligence which is Supreme. Even I had to drop it somewhere along the way because the thoughts that stepped into my mind like moonlight from a window, were of a nature and type that I could not hear them inside and remain functional in the world— have something Kapur Saab, I have made these snacks with such love and affection. Our talk can go on.' Kaptan Saab patted me affectionately.

' What single day are you referring to Kaptan Saab?' I asked

'It is the festival of Holi in north India when people rub colour into the faces and bodies of each other. They eat concoctions made out of bhang (dried leaves of the marijuana plant) and sing and dance, and make much merriment. I'm sure you must be familiar with it. Usually however the marijuana concoctions are too strong or too weak, neither of which lead to a controlled experience. I too was a lone adventurer. After I had been introduced to marijuana and hashish (the resin from the marijuana plant) I was left by my co-adventurers to find my own way in the wide and most unpredictable world of marijuana. Well I took it on as something that would benefit me, somehow. As time went on north India saw something of an invasion by the foreigners who called themselves ' hippies' and went about carrying smoking pipes of clay around their necks.

I smoked with many of them but found them to be somewhat argumentative, and somewhat vacuous. I thought that they should remain with the dried marijuana leaves rather than inhaling hashish or taking the flowering tops thick in resin (ganja). Their capacity is good with a light dose of oriental marijuana, a strong dose impairs their capacity to think logically. Of course now we are at the fag end of the hippie invasion and one does not see them in these areas any more.' Kaptan Saab trailed off looking beyond my shoulders at the windows which gave a faint ethereal image of the snows through the lamplight in the room where we were seated across the table.

It occurred to me to ask Kaptan Saab at that point in time about my plans for the house. I told him that I had barely six months with me, and of these almost three would be the cold months when construction in the mountains is slowed down considerably because the whole process becomes very uncomfortable with freezing winds blowing, and the annual snowfall also taking it's toll. Kaptan Saab assured me that the major portion of the construction would be over by then and only a few assortments would be left by the time six months were over. I discussed with him the overall strategy of carting slate and quarrying stone, apart from the woodwork. He assured me that the workers in that part of the world were as good as the best. The whole plan it was clear was hinged on the management of the workers and keeping them in good humor. For this it was more than obvious to me that there should be a steady flow of money coming to me which I could disburse to the workers for their labours.

Kaptan Saab was a practical man, and he assured me that none of the supplies would be bogged down, and he made his own modest claim for a retainer, in lieu of the help he was rendering me, which he said generously enough, I could give him towards the end of the project, when the house was nearing completion. Meanwhile there were problems galore with the construction of the house, which I liked to think of as the temple house. In fact I had seriously thought at that stage of staying in one room and a dressing room, while converting the other one into a temple with icons of Siva and Kali. The remaining room could be converted into a kitchen. However I was not so sure about all this and it was a tentative idea. It was tentative because I would then have to think of committing my entire life to religion per se, and not just to studying it intensively.

As the experienced person would already have observed being a priest in a temple is quite different from asking questions from a priest in a temple. Not that there were no examples in that region of foreigners having settled down to a religious life and having made something out of it. And in fact if I wanted to make a career out of spirituality there was more than enough good land further east on the huge ridge, which was part of the village but yet unpopulated. The thought of starting an ashram, a holy abode of believers, entered my mind, but I could not clinch down this idea because I felt that my vocation in life was not yet the spiritual life in it's formal sense. I wanted to be spiritually realized but remain like my mentors, out of the limelight as far as possible because being in the front often creates problems in practicing spirituality.

We said the prayers on the land on which the house was being built with a Brahmin priest and the digging of the foundation started on a bright auspicious day with a few wisps of clouds lingering in the sky. The soil was soft with years of cultivation having cleared off any huge chunks of stones, or even little ones. On the snow mountains side of it the foundation went down upto seven feet before solid ground could be found. On the other sides too the foundation was unusually deep. This meant that the rock and stones quarried nearby literally went in by the heap and was swallowed whole by the ground. But there was no help for it, except to enthuse that if a second floor ever went up the house would be standing on a solid foundation.

I am talking of the building of this temple house in some detail because at that stage in my life I was seriously in a dilemma. I wondered seriously whether giving up everything in the world was the right step for me to take. I had got so far as to be on my way making a house, and even thinking of turning over half of it to prayer and worship. I would have to take the responsibility of keeping the temple portion clean. Further it was also obvious to me that that at some point in time I would have to shift eastward into a much larger estate while the house was converted and renovated into a temple. Being where it was would make it an excellent site for a temple, especially that of Siva and Kali, since the snow mountain dedicated to them was bang in front of the temple house with nothing in between except the deep valleys which rose in row after row until they gained enough in height to be part of the eternal snows themselves.

Yet I kept mulling this idea, with the alternative one of having a relationship with the mountains but not a total one. This attracted me more as the time went on because I felt that I did not have too many people who had my specialized interests in religion and spirituality. The few people that I could discuss issues of spirituality were few and far between. Sri Turiya had virtually confessed that he had other things to contemplate rather than my special problems. The other yogis that I met had been interesting but peripatetic so that I could not follow them very far. Meanwhile the power of Maya had awakened within me and it was I who was keeping it at bay to some extent. This was in fact the main area of conflict. Each time I meditated I gazed into the wonder of a world of imagination in which the beautiful and gorgeous Maya shifted in and out and when with the force of my concentration I could focus on her completely, she would look at me and smile. That smile was enough and in one of my meditations I found that she was waiting for me to talk.

' Am I going to stay in the mountains forever?' I asked Maya.

'You are not really interested in externalities beyond a certain point. Depending on which way your life goes you would not be averse to staying in the mountains for chunks of your life. However, I sense that over the years the sense of mingling with people and the anonymity offered by the big cities will attract you much more than the fame that the mountains can create for those who live among them. Moreover you are leaving you mark behind. A single room has already been constructed on that land and you wake up with the sun kissing the tips of the peaks. It cannot get any better, as you have no one to disturb your chain of thought. In many ways this is a peak of experience which you will have to look back into to share with other people, and to understand in a deeper way. I am a simple deity, first born of Brahman, who delegated all creation to me. There is no 'you', and no 'me', we are parts of the same reality. Then how come you can contact me and talk to me like human beings talk to each other face to face, and the next person cannot. I am not telling you something that you don't know. Your entire existential experience from life to life has brought you nearer and nearer to me. And this is the point: with your house being built rapidly you realize that you don't want to be a hero. This means that you cannot stay in the mountains and follow your plans. I am always with you and there is no precondition that you have to live in the mountains or the plains so far as I am concerned. So, my friend, I am the dilemma in your life, not the mountains, snows, people, or even your studies. You are not able to decide what exactly you would like to do with your life. I'll give you a simple solution — let it drift and you will automatically find out for yourself which way you want to go.' Maya gave a dazzling smile and shook her head literally mesmerizing me with her feminine beauty.

'I think perhaps I don't want to grapple with reality. I think that you have made me weak and spoilt with your cascades of love and affection. I want somehow to avoid taking responsibility for anyone apart from myself. This I realize is totally against the tenor and basis of the eternal religion, and I am aware that the tenets of the eternal religion cannot and should not be violated at any cost. So theoretically I am sound, but it is my body that shakes at the thought of having to live in the noise, dust, heat, and confusion of the plains. Strangely that is where the most activity is situated even in terms of some occupation that one would have to take up. What exactly this will be is something very difficult to guess for a job in the university is by no means a certainty. All this makes me feel that I should cover my head with my meditation blanket and forget everyone and everything'. I had spoken intensely and emotionally to Maya and I saw that she was amused. This amusement of hers at my outbursts always perplexed me. What other people found threatening, even provocative and frightening, was for Maya, a gentle breeze in the evening.

'There is nothing to it', said Maya calling me by name, ' It is just the mists of time that you are encountering. In some time they will clear away and you will find that there is nothing to really debate and think about. I would also suggest that you use the time you spend at the site of the house to gather notes for your study, as these workers are the people who have this knowledge. When you can go and witness the exorcist rituals,which take place almost everyday and try to figure out your presentation. This will help you keep track of your work instead of thinking on what anyone would call a pretty wild trajectory of imagination. Why I don't drop in on you too often is because I am going to be with you forever, after a while. This intervening period has to be crossed and it will be excruciatingly painful. It will be full of experiences that you can hardly relate so strange are they that they will have to be kept away in the recesses of your mind until I come back to you to dissect or delete them, so to speak'. Maya's voice drifted lazily like incense smoke in a still room and I floated along with it. I was having a premonition of what would happen to me once I left the hills and I perspired profusely. The only solace that I could draw from those visions was they are seemed to end on a 'normal' note rather than a bizarre one. I was glad as I looked into the beyond that the latter part of my life would be a psychological adventure, and would have little to do with personally supervising the building of spiritual community centres and so on which had been earlier part of my thoughts. This was certainly a relief and I parted that evening from Maya with a wave of the hand. She waved back usually and if in a good mood she would even blow me a benediction. She who was the eldest daughter of Brahman looked so frail and young, and was so spiritually enticing that I found it a bit ridiculous to try any other way to signal the end of a session.

So it was Maya who really resolved my dilemma, and gave me sufficient warning for the adjustment that I would have to face when I returned from the mountains. Once I knew that a trying period lay ahead I wanted to make as much of my time as possible with the mountain people. I had begun to get a feeling that I might not return, and that if I did it would not be in the same circumstances. I realized above all that this was the time I had better put my mind to researching any rituals in the area because I had understood I would not be returning as a researcher. Maybe a tourist, but then who knew about that either ? These feelings and thoughts made me very sentimental and nostalgic in the last six months of my stay in the mountains. No people had ever looked so beautiful to me, nor given me so much love.

In fact I was the uncrowned King of that region and I was treated like a monarch wherever I went. My people, as I fondly think of them never let me lose sleep thinking that if any threat came nobody would help. In fact I was sleeping peacefully in that village without even locking my door.

One day late in the evening, I met Kaptan Saab, and as was usual we would go for a ' talkie-walkie' in which he taught me some aspect of ancient wisdom. That evening I was in a different kind of mood. I felt a little reckless and this is what enabled me to breach the topic around one type of vaporous bodies, the bhuts and the pretas. This latter two categories were associated along every nook and cranny of the hill lanes. Clearly they are a type of vapourous body which can't go out of the place of domicile. Thus the Kaptan pointed out to me that the later life in this universe takes place in a vapourous or misty shape. Sometime it is in the form of spirals of mud and even as an unending unyielding breeze on the balcony, even when everything is still.Now to me the very idea of vapourous bodies caught on and started to puzzle me greatly. I was determined to get at the bottom of this riddle. The first opportunity that I got I confronted Kaptan Saab.

'Tell me Kaptan Saab, what are these vapourous bodies that everyone here is so often talking about. Are they real or are they imaginary?'

'It takes some degree of imagination to actually see

a bhut or pret in the initial stages, but with time the firmness comes when we can visualize these spirits to perfection. The important point is that there has been a change of energy. The energy of the bhut or preta goes into the viewer and then he or she is spiritually strengthened. On the other hand the bhut is recharged with living energy. In dreams we meet people with whom we plan short term, long term, and indeed frame to frame.

'So these entities that have crossed beyond death, apart from personal experience, they are the only direct source of whether life after death is really there or not.Without their divine intervention nothing can happen. I think these forms of vapourous energy have been misunderstood badly and dismissed as unimportant, or worse still, useless. As such these willing helpers were put in cold storage since medieval times, and not used to consult for anything, even matters of the spirit unless one locates the bhut and establishes a that interaction will have deemed to be held as redundant and useless............'

I butted into his ruminations, from which there seemed to be no respite. If one was with Kaptan Saab it was a time full of fun and frolic, and of feeling secure in the densely wooded environment. I was surprised when Kaptan Saab turned to me and said with a smile,

'I was hoping that you would turn to this topic of disembodied beings or vapourous bodies and shed some light on their existence. I am really fascinated by this area of the afterworld. I mean only through the existence of a ghost can we be sure that indeed we don't really die but change.' I listened to him patiently.

'My friend, you don't seem to realize that very many people are themselves bhut and preta. They have borrowed so much shakti (power) that they actually settle down and have children and so on. I mean I know several of them and from vapourous bodies they have entered into a child or even a young person. Age has nothing to do with it. It is a question of purchasing time on earth, which is populated by physical beings, rather than vapourous ones. So the strongest evidence on bhuts is that we can form linkages which never get lost, once they are firm. It is through these linkages that we set ourselves up in the land of vapourous bodies. If we believe in the spirits of our ancestors we find that the ancestors start solving our problems. We may not even know or acknowledge but the ancestors then take control. Between the ancestors and the inheritor, so to speak is the area of the whole of life. The whole of life is busy making merry while the fun lasts. Every one is deeply aware how much they can afford and how much they can't. The problem is that no one wants to share their experience and in doing so they undo the good luck.

'Wherever we go we don't go by ourselves. Our entire lineage of ancestors whose reprresentative we are comes with us. Each interaction is a friendly or enemy combat. There is no chance at all of entering into Moksa without the energy. There is no hope at all of entering swarga or heaven without the help of the bhuts and the pretas, that is why they are worshipped in each Ganesh puja or prayer. Kaptan Saab became silent as if lost in some labyrinth of thought. I put my hand on his shoulder and consoled him, but he was in no mood for reconciliation.

'I'm upset because I revealed to you an oral Vedic secret. Our departed ones are all with us. We need a little flexibility of the human code of perception to be able to acknowledge with our logic that yes perceptually we have connected many a time with the other world. Then it is ignorance of this fact that excites fear and curiosity, when it is something we have to work upon, you know?' Kaptan was inconsolable and I asked him to clarify this alarming turn of events.

'This is the secret of secrets and I have revealed it to you. We are no better or worse off in the afterworld, than here. Yes peoples fortunes go up and down, with the karmas that they have accumulated. We should imagine that there is redemption for us in the form of eternal rest. We are worker's in a universe where no one can rest without devotion or prayer, even obsession with someone or something.' Kaptan Saab was wiping the sweat from his neck.

'Now I am done for', he said. 'If I know you one day you will make use of all this and by that time my bhut will be with you. Would you mind if I lived in your vicinity and helped you accomplish your goals in this world and the next?'. I was in a reckless mood and offered him unconditional residence at the house we were building which he accepted without hesitation, even with gratitude. He expressed quite clearly that he liked the location of the field that we were building the house. He said he loved the view of the valleys and mountains from there, and that it would be the perfect location for him to stay in a vapourous body after his physical self turned into the elements of the universe and recombined after his funeral into the vapourous body. I was so secure and comfortable with him and admired him so much that I felt he was doing me a favour and not the other way round.

The catch was of course that one was working on the premise of the after life being there.

I found that the tactic of changing the subject worked here.I asked him a general question.

'When do you think a person is ready for spiritual instructions?' I said with intense curiosity.

'As soon as the little one begins to walk the inner spiritual atmosphere begins to develop rapidly. The parents' spiritual atmosphere begins to suffuse into the psyche of the child and the seed is sown by the parents behaviour and habits. You may find it unbelievable but I can remember my birth and all that followed it with complete clarity. In fact I was aware of my parents' harmony of behaviour even in the womb'. He was utterly serious

'Do you mean to say that influences enter into the womb itself – then when does spiritual development really start?'

'The impressions begin in the womb but they really come in huge waves once the child is a bit steady on the feet. This is because to learn to gain motor control often makes the child invest all the energy for that purpose alone. Later when that motor control is gained energy is freed for other purposes, including the quest for realization'. Kaptan Saab was getting out of his solemn mood and began to laugh and smile.

'You know it is very difficult to believe that man survives in a vapourous body after death of the physical body. This realization alone can set man free. So long as we think we are the physical body realization can never come to a person. Even if we are theoretically convinced about the vapourous body it takes a training of years before we are convinced about it's actual existence'. Kaptan Saab smiled at me in a paternal way and clapped me on the back as if we were in the same boat. I told him regarding my gazing experiences and about my meditations on Maya hoping to hear his views.

'I have been gazing at a flame for years together and have seen the unthinkable through the world that opened up to me through its inner core. You don't have to convince me about the vapourous body. I know it exists since often I have left my physical and gone into the realm of vapourous bodies and the other world. I also seem to think that it is not possible for everyone in the world to be enlightened because this knowledge is for the select few. I deliberately wanted you to comment on this mysterious facet of our lives on earth. What would you say ?' I waited for his comment as we looked on to the ice mountains slowly turning crimson in the distance.

'A little knowledge is very dangerous because it makes us feel reckless and complete, when actually we are the furthest thing from being so. I think your gazing experiences have just begun and judging from your encounters the really great adventures in this field still lie ahead. Do you know that it is possible to dream in a sequence so that the dark side of awareness is lighted up and awareness is always with us ?' Kaptan Saab smiled and his face was lighted up with an unearthly light bouncing off the snow peaks. In fact I had never seen anything like the sunsets from the ridge on the village. Everything became incandescent and filled with a spiritual glow.

'Do you mean to say that such a person never sleeps?' I asked in some consternation.

'Only a very little of the dark side of awareness is retained and it is life as usual for such a person, whether he is aware in this world or aware in the other world. For such a person it is a small step from this world to the next and the power to leave the physical body develops to the point that when the time comes the physical is just dropped away like an old leaf . That is the greatest gift of a matured awareness. Death becomes a natural process, and life is on the other side. We are located in one of many states of awareness and the other world is a way of speaking about many new possibilities that awaken with enlightenment. This is not our quest but a byproduct of our meditation.' Kaptan Saab looked at me affectionately and the surroundings had by now become suffused with the moonlight in the valley below and all around us.

'What you are actually saying is that if we have the power, the shakti, we need never leave the earth?' I asked in growing excitement and anticipation.

' It becomes optional for us to visit the vibration of the earth and to observe whatever we want, including near and dear ones. In fact it is seldom realized that we can actually direct the flow of events from the other side. Many of the inexplicable decisions that are taken in people's lives are in fact taken by someone who is not physically present, but the awareness is existent. Keep in mind however the fact that not very many people attain such heights of spirituality as to be able to affect even outcomes between nations. However there are many who do retain their awareness and can direct the outcome of events sheerly out of the power of their spiritual awareness. Do you understand ?' Kaptan Saab looked at me quizzingly.

'I'm not so sure whether I understand fully but it fits in with the wisdom of the ancients which is enshrined in the Vedas, especially in the forest teachings. I guess you're right! Not everyone can make it happen but some can !'

Kaptan Saab stood up and I followed him down to his house which was downhill from where the construction was taking place. We were to have dinner together that night. Kaptan knew I was vegetarian but I told him that I would not mind him cooking something non-vegetarian for himself. The conversations continued in the house over dinner. I had to eat a bit slowly, as usual for me in his presence. The food was well cooked and I enjoyed every morsel.

'Are we saying it is possible to live forever?' I asked him.

'I am saying that death as we conceive of it is

unreality, and does not happen. The solace that man has when he thinks of his ultimate death is in fact hopeful thinking in the extreme. We move bed and baggage to the world most suited to us at the time of death. So to hope that death is the great release from toil and trouble is a vain idea. It just doesn't happen like that!' Kaptan Saab dug into his meat with gusto and I watched him fascinated. He was getting on in the years and his talking so objectively regarding his death made a shiver go down my back.

'I suppose it requires guts to even contemplate what you have said let alone the possibility of accepting it'. I was aghast at the dimensions he had opened up for me in the realm of thought.

'Do you recommend some kind of meditation for me to come to terms with reality a bit better. I have been gazing at the candle flame but I think I could try something else if it is recommended by you ?'.

'No. Don't worry about it. Your gazing meditation will itself give you an answer. And your ishta devi, Maya will herself take care of it. In fact it was obviously her who arranged it in such a way that you came to this village. I will not interfere with her, as she is a great goddess. But I do understand that you have asked this question in a spirit of enquiry, and that is permissible.' We were both silent for a while. I understood what he meant. Goddess Maya would always be with me and it was only through her that I would be able to contact Kaptan Saab in the other world.

'In my meditation I have been getting indications that I should now start winding up my affairs in Devagiri and head back to Delhi. I have even got a letter that I should do precisely this from my professor. There are so many loose ends and patches to my data that I shudder to think what will be my fate.' I spoke earnestly since I was seeking some kind of hint as to what I should do with the time left to me in the village.

'It would be better if you can drag some time out from the construction of the house and look into the areas you feel are still to be investigated. In any case it is natural for you to feel this way. I have spent all my life in the hills, and I have told you what I could regarding your work. I think that no one can go to a village and understand everything about it without worrying about it being complete. I would go so far as to say that even the villagers do not understand their own life in the village in its wholeness. That is the total interconnections between what is happening in the village and in the region. I have helped you gather your data and I think you could paint a good picture of what is happening here so far as the religious and spiritual side is concerned. It would be better if you stop worrying and fill in the gaps with the help of the construction workers.' Kaptan Saab looked at me querying my response.

'My problem is that that I have a lot of material on the spiritual side. Then there are the exorcist rituals of various types, the rituals of birth, marriage and death, the various dominant myths and legends. What is lacking is the problem of the lower groups and I intend to cover that thoroughly in the time left to me to be here.' I was voicing my innermost thoughts and Kaptan Saab gave me a patient hearing.

'What you are saying is alright, but not quite to the point. I have known you long enough to be able to tell you that what you are hearing is not the imagination of the villagers. The supernatural exists here in this village and region as a very solid reality. Tonight you will get a taste of it. Don't worry no harm will come to you but you should keep calm and not react no matter what happens'. Kaptan Saab broke off his observation suddenly leaving me in a state of agitation.

'What exactly do you mean by all this ? I'm very apprehensive of what you are saying. Frankly I'm not interested in going any deeper into the matters that I have already covered. I believe the villagers when they say the entire village is teeming with supernatural beings.........'

'That is alright, my friend, don't worry about it. Do you really think that theoretical inputs will help you to get to the root of the problem. You have to be convinced that what you are hearing is absolutely true. It is not a figment of anyone's imagination. Tonight you will know for sure'. Kaptan was in a rare mood that night and this made me all the more apprehensive. I felt he had something that he was hiding from me. I took leave of him that night with a sense of sheer despondency. On the other hand I was curious about what was going to happen to me. I decided to do some flame gazing meditation on a lamp that I had picked up from an antique shop in a nearby village to steady myself. However my usual concentration was lacking. The flame steadied my nerves but I was not quite myself.

It was already quite cold and I covered myself with a quilt and kept completely quiet. I slipped off to sleep and was woken by some wind rapping at the door. In my drowsiness I had forgotten or only half remembered what Kaptan had said. As I turned over in my bed I saw a ray of light flashing through the gauze curtains of the door. It was as if someone was walking on the field above the house with a powerful flashlight. But at this late hour in the night.? I remembered in a moment of sheer perplexion that this could be what Kaptan had referred to. And as I watched the movement of the light I realized that it was moving straight like the beam of a locomotive. There was no indication at all that it could be a man masquerading as a supernatural being. The possibility of Kaptan having set someone up for my benefit entered my mind briefly, but he had no stakes in such a venture.

As these thoughts moved through my mind the light became a double beam, one larger than the other and passed by the house. I consoled myself that perhaps it was some villager taking that path late at night. This explanation was not tenable. That field was not a short cut to any other place and was rather more hazardous than the normal path. Being a little drowsy I was not yet agitated. I dismissed the episode as being something inexplicable. I turned over in my bed and tried to sleep but sleep would not come to me.

Suddenly and very softly I began to hear someone or something walking inside the area of the house that was still under construction. At first I thought it was a stray dog, but what would a stray dog have to do with an area where there was nothing for it to eat. I heard the heavy breath of a large animal and got into a mood in which I was ready for anything to happen. The 'thing' moved around for a while and I expected the connecting door to be rammed any moment. It even entered my mind that this large animal with it's heavy breathing could be a man eating tiger. Then it struck me suddenly that the lights that I had seen earlier and this animal which was moving softly but ominously were related. I was cold with fear because the house next to mine was hundreds of yards away and I was alone. Then from the northern side I heard a stone slam into the wall just below the unprotected window. A few yards to the left and it would have shattered the window and I did not hear anyone laugh or curse. The crux of the matter was that at well past midnight I could not imagine anyone being upto such tricks for the sheer sake of convincing me about supernatural beings.

After what seemed an eternity silence prevailed and the sound of the insects chirping began to come through.

Exhausted by the tension of the events I went to sleep and woke up early in the morning. I found nothing in the area to either confirm or negate what I had experienced the night before. Moreover the experience had been so private that I could not even discuss it with anyone. Yet I understood more deeply than before that there were experiences of the villagers that they could not talk about without appearing to be dim witted or wacky to the other person. Such experiences I learned latter were the stuff which the deities of the area were responsible for.

The house construction got going again after a lull of a couple of months when it had got held up due to paucity of funds. My work also went forward step by step and at long last I was able to develop a strategy for the presentation of my case. The weather had turned bitterly cold and I felt chilly under my large quilt even when the fire was going in the fireplace. This was the time when my spiritual experiences in the village began to explode in my brain with regular intensity. The rarified air, the ice mountains, and my regular meditation had produced a very light headed feeling in me and I found it difficult to think linearly.

At this point in time I got an opportunity to visit a dak bungalow that was supposed to be haunted. The villager who offered to take me there said it was a place worth visiting. I was not excited with the prospect of seeing bhuts or ghosts but had the day off as there were no construction activities on the house that day. It was nearing the end of my stay in the mountains. I did not know that this was going to be my last stretch in that village for any length in time. The route we took us away and beyond the village temple and I found that my guide had a good knowledge of the lie of the land. We talked casually on the way and he mentioned that in the old days only a select few people wanted to stay at the spot we were visiting and did this for shikar.

We spent a while drinking tea at one of his cousins house on the way situated in what seemed literally to be a gully. How it had been built there was a mystery to me for it was all of two stories high and the folks seemed completely cut off. I remembered a similar trip I had made earlier in the year with a village acquaintance. That had decidedly been less frightening than this one. After a while on the trail we didn't see anyone and when we decided to rest for a while my guide told me that we couldn't stay put for too long as we had to be back by the evening. Meanwhile he showed me how to construct a smoking pipe built into the earth with a bamboo stem coming out of the hole. It was a peculiar contraption which actually worked and fascinated me. I took a few drags from this improvised hookah. We then went into total desolation. The jungle around was thick and the trail enough for two people at a time sometimes becoming too thin to take even two persons side by side. We had to take a loop before we would reach the dak bungalow which was shaped like an inverted U. When we finally reached the dak bungalow I was totally fascinated by the view from the verandah. There were little hills sloping away into the blue of the sky and they looked golden yellow where the sun fell on them and were wooded with trees that had never been thinned or cut. I could not believe where I was and that such a spot existed in the hills. It was possible to be at that bungalow and not feel at all intimidated by the scenery. In fact it appeared to be in the middle of nowhere. I vowed to come back again but I knew at that very moment that perhaps this was not possible. We looked for the chowkidar of the bungalow but he was not to be found. We spent some time on the verandah sitting with our legs dangling from the raised platform. I mention this incident because this was one of those places in the mountains that had a charm all of it's own. Having got there one didn't feel like leaving that spot so beautiful and comfortable was it to the senses and perception. I toyed with the idea of spending the night there but my guide informed me that this was not feasible. I was adamant. I knew that due to my unannounced visits to some neighbouring towns for construction materials I would not be missed in Devagiri. I asked my guide to stay with me and that we would go the next day but for some reason he started quaking with fear. His was certainly not a normal response to the lovely view and the quiet surroundings. In my bag I had carried some candles and a little food. I told him that we could share it. I also told him that the chowkidar was bound to come back sooner or later and that we could very conveniently get a comfortable place to pass the night. I desperately wanted to see the sunrise on those benign mountain ranges. I was sure it would be the experience of a lifetime.

When the local guide who had come with me realized that I was adamant in my stand he wished me well and made off in the direction we had come from. It must be said to his credit that he did volunteer one last time to take me along.I told him that I would find my way back although it was deep in the jungle. Something in that little nook in the vast mountains had totally infatuated me and made me lose all sense of logic and proportion.

Hardly had the guide gone round the corner that the chowkidar appeared with a load of wood. Despite my casual clothes he took me for an officer in the forest department.We exchanged greetings and he said that no one had come to that bungalow now ever since he could remember and he had been maintaining it from the grant he got for it when he made his monthly trip to the District headquarters to collect his meagre salary. He assured me that I would pass as much time as I liked comfortably and that he would provide for me so far as board and lodging were concerned. He said that he had a kitchen garden which was yielding potatoes and other vegetables and that I should relax. I did so and stretched out on the verandah itself with my shawl over my shoulders to watch the glorious sunset. So infatuated was I with the beauty of the changing colours that I did not even feel the cold of the winter wind that evening. Meanwhile the chowkidar got busy making the meal and organizing the bed. When that sunset had slowly slipped into a moonlit night I thought that I had seen all there was to be seen, and I was literally ready to die. The changing hues and the lingering effect of the cold breeze had given me an experience in the mountains that I would never forget as long as I lived. Till this day I long for that little bungalow and the small hill ranges surrounding it.

I was little prepared for what happened thereafter. When I had eaten of the repast cooked by the chowkidar he looked at me with a slant in the eyes. Suddenly I felt the icy claws of fear grab my entrails.

'Sahib', he said, 'the reason none comes to this bungalow is because the house has the ghost of the Memsahib. She came here soon after this bungalow was built to stay with her lover. The lover ran away and the Memsahib drank some poison and killed herself. Maybe you will see her tonight. That is the reason why your friend ran away. Are you afraid of bhuts ? If you are please tell me and I will stay with you all through the night and we will keep awake !' The chowkidar's voice trembled with fear.

'How come you stay here all alone in such conditions?' I asked in some consternation but not really comprehending the full impact of what he was saying. The scenery on that moonlit night was so mesmerizing that I felt capable of anything, even facing a bhut if necessary.

'Don't worry Sahib', said the chowkidar ' Memsahib is a very beautiful and kind bhut. She has not harmed me and will not harm you. The problem with me is that I do not know how to speak her language and she knows very little of mine. So we cannot talk every much. I am sure you will like her. She is very sensitive and is probably already aware that you are here. If you can keep your fright in check and treat her like a normal person she might even tell you something of great use to you. After all she is a bhut who has now lived more than a hundred years, and roamed all over the mountains. She is really very gentle and kind'.

'Is this something which happens with everybody who comes here?' I asked.

'Nobody has come here in the last ten years or more. This type of sylvan isolation with little wooded hills all around, does not appeal to very many people. Then it is pretty out of the way and there is no hint of civilization. I like to think of the Memsahib as the presiding deity of this place who likes to know what is happening'. The chowkidar was rubbing his hands hard together to keep off the growing cold.

'Would it be possible to put up a few logs in the fireplace, to keep the room warm ?' I asked hopefully.

'I will gladly do that sahib. You must now get ready for your food so that you can go to sleep in preparation for the Memsahib.' The chowkidar appeared to be nervous.

'How will I see the Memsahib if I go to sleep?' I asked in surprise.

'Don't worry about all that. All that matters is that you are not to think of her as an ordinary bhut. She is as much a living creature as you or me. In fact she has been with awareness longer than you or me in this form.'

I was tired by this time and had put on an additional

jacket from my bag and watched the chowkidar set up the logs in the fireplace. I ate the chappatis, lentils, and fried potatoes that he gave me in a large brass plate with relish, and then climbed into one of the two beds that had been set up. I was very exhausted and had a few brief moments of clarity before I simply blacked out into deep sleep. I was not aware of what was happening to me and had completely forgotten that there was any place like the one I was in.

Then in the depths of the night I felt someone or something lightly tapping the razai with a light touch. I thought that it was a moth that had somehow got into the room and pulled the comforter over my head. However the light flapping continued at brief intervals. I looked out from under the comforter at the moonlight bathed room. At the far end near the window which was closed sat a fair woman with an evening gown. Her eyes were violet and her hair was golden and she could not have been more than eighteen years old. There wasn't a wrinkle on her oval face. There was no doubt about it she was a beautiful young woman.

I threw caution to the winds and gently got up from the bed keeping the razai around my shoulders.

'Hello', I said to the woman with a smile. Strangely I felt at ease with her and not apprehensive in the slightest bit. She told me her name was Rubina and that she had been alive since the Indian Mutiny of 1857 when she was already in her teens. She said she had come up to camp in these areas which were almost totally inaccessible in those days with a male friend. That friend was killed in the Mutiny and she was left alone to wander the hills.She said she had lived with a shepherd family who looked after her as their own and when she had left for her heavenly abode she found that on death she was back in the utopian valley.

'In fact', she said, ' no one who comes to this place

would like to leave it, it is so gentle and beautiful. I offer you my help and my company if you want to come here after your time comes .... Is that a deal ?' Rubina's cheeks dimpled as she smiled. I found that if she was a bhut my entire ideas of bhuts was based on wrong presumptions. I had always thought of bhuts as malignant entities that lived on threatening others and creating trouble for them. I said as much to Rubina.

'I was under the impression that supernatural beings from the other world were troublemakers, but you completely contradict this idea. You are obviously very kind, beautiful and helpful and are not taking any advantage out of me and my situation. I am virtually at your mercy but you talk the language of love, gentleness, kindness and compassion. I am sorry that when the chowkidar was talking about the Memsahib I visualized some dangerous type of entity which would threaten me and lay down conditions. That hasn't happened and I'm very glad.' I had almost a crush on Rubina by now so soft and cultured did I find her.

'Have you any particular plan you want to follow here?' she asked gently pushing back her golden hair.

'I want to watch the sunrise at this place. I'm sure it will be tremendous. I want to watch this sunrise as if it were the first and the last sunrise that I have ever seen. Do you have any suggestions ?' I looked deeply into her violet eyes.

'The question is whether you want to include the snows in your perception or see the sunrise in the seclusion of this utopia? If you want to see it along with the snows we would have to walk some way from here. Otherwise we just go into the verandah.' She was quite relaxed.

'What about you ? Will you also be with me, or not?' I asked in anticipation.

'I'd love to be with you but as the moonlight fades and the sunrise comes I become invisible as I am of the moon and my body is woven in moonbeams. So as morning comes I will leave you and the sunrise will be totally your own. An experience to cherish for a lifetime, and you know that I will do what I can and should to make your life on earth as happy and pleasant as possible. Don't worry ! I like you !' Rubina was positively radiant as she said that. I found myself getting sentimental, romantic and emotional and we spent the rest of the night talking about ourselves and our lives . I never felt that I was talking to a supernatural being except for the fact that there was an inner glow on her face as if a light were shining from within, making her radiant.

At a certain point in the night I found that Rubina was getting a bit restless and I enquired why this was so.

' It's a question of luminescence, especially that of the sun.It's not good for beings like me so we have to retreat when the day is approaching and go back into our cocoons and relax. The point is when the sun is up the moonlight cannot be seen, nor can we. It's like going to sleep. We have our gnarled tree trunks or gullies or a cave in the mountains and we can go there. If the place is dark enough we can continue our existence as if the sun had not arisen. It's not a punishment and the day passes pleasantly and as we want it to, but many prefer to rest in slumber, in a dark quiet place in the hills, trees, caves, and so on.' Rubina was at her engaging best, and I was fascinated. What confused me completely was the fact that she was just like any other person I knew except for the fact that she spoke English whereas most of the people I had come across in the village did not understand it.

'Will I see you again ?' I asked.

'If you come here again, you will. Otherwise we can meet in your gazing meditations where you meet the great goddess who is truly the last word so far as our world is concerned. We are but particles of dust in front of her. I wonder if you would like to touch up with me again?' Rubina gave a brief sigh and held my gaze with her violet eyes.

'I must go' continued Rubina and leave you alone for a while. Try to get some rest because the sunrise here is special and you should be fresh for it. I have some work to do and have been putting it off.'

'What kind of work are you talking about?' I asked somewhat surprised.

'Do you think we don't have practical tasks in our world ?' she said in surprise. 'To tell you the truth our world is full to the brim with work of various sorts and it keeps us busy. So busy that we rarely try to make contact with the other world, the world of men'. Rubina moved away from the seat near the window and waved a thin white hand as if to say goodbye and literally slid out of the wire meshing in the window as if she were made of mist or smoke. I found myself alone in the room feeling very lonely as Rubina's presence had more than filled up the space with her radiance. I was caught in an emotional trap and saw to my consternation that there were still a few hours before sunrise. I did not particularly feel like doing anything. The thought that I should gaze into the candles I had brought with me crossed my mind but I was too excited to go through that procedure which required a calm and controlled mind. I forced myself to rest and lay down in the bed. Before I knew it I was asleep and woke up only when the birds were chirruping. A vast luminescence filled the sky though no single ray of light was visible. The entire area of the hills was lit up as if with a hidden source of light. Later the sunrays came over the hills opposite the bungalow and barely touched the high tops of the trees surrounding the bungalow. The light was a deep yellow and tinged with blue. All the time the birdsong went on unabated and this lasted all of an hour with hundreds of birds joining in. It was a truly remarkable morning. The chowkidar came with some tea and food which I ate. I squared my accounts with him, thanked him, and was on my way. The chowkidar accompanied me till the crucial bend or loop in the route. Beyond that I went along myself and saw no one till I was in the vicinity of Devagiri.

Kaptan had enquired about me and he had been informed that I had gone to see the Bhut Bungalow and when I met him he asked whether I had met the bhut of the bungalow.I told him that I had but that the meeting could not be described. In turn I asked him whether he had ever been there and he said he had been there some fifteen years earlier. His problem was that he didn't understand English and that the Memsahib didn't know much Hindi, so they couldn't talk very much to each other except exchange pleasantries.

Meanwhile Kaptan told me that the consignment of slates that I had ordered had arrived from the District capital and that the laying of the roof and the floor could be started. We had managed to get long beams of wood for the roof so that we could fill in the gaps with wood chips and then lay the slates on clay mud. We did all the necessary ceremonies before laying down the roof and the floor but inclement weather stopped us from filling in the roof of one of the rooms and the verandah.

A snow storm was brewing up and it was obvious that one should have a supply of wood to burn in the hearth and to keep the room warm. I stocked up on flour and potatoes apart from getting a supply of wood slivers. Then without warning the snow flakes began to fall. Slowly at first and then with greater regularity and density. This was the first snowfall I had seen in many a year and I was fascinated. I walked after the first days snow to the end of the field and looked at the house which looked like a newly decked up bride. It would never look prettier and more becoming and I took it in knowing that perhaps it would not be in my fate to see the house again like that. The snow on the beams and on the logs on the roof gave the house a surreal look and I was overwhelmed with emotion. In my mind there could not be a better location for a temple house where a scholar could lead a reclusive life dedicating himself to the cause of the eternal religion. In that week of snowfall I ate fried potatoes with thick unleavened bread and ghee, and when I had to drink something apart from water I made myself some fresh coffee. No one visited me for seven days and I was grateful for this respite, though I did feel that if anything had happened to me there was no one who cared. In fact this shocked me deeply and I began to feel deep within that I was truly an outsider 'looking in', and that maybe my perception of 'belonging' was at best wishful thinking.

I began planning to get back to Delhi. I had already got a brief letter from my professor in Delhi saying there had to be a beginning a middle, and an end to field work. It was already early into 1981 and I now planned to wind up my work in Devagiri and go back to collate my data in Delhi. It remained for me to wait for an appropriate opportunity to meditate and gaze on Maya and see what she had to say. I took the first opportunity to set up a session in the room of the house that was complete, relatively speaking.

It was a late dark night in the middle of January 1981 that I set the lamp that I had bought in an antique shop to a low wick and put it against the wall. I seated myself opposite the lamp and tried to see whether the situation was suitable for gazing. Finding the situation was not exactly right I shifted the lamp onto the window sill which faced the snows. The thin curtains swayed a bit in the breeze and the wall was very dimly lit giving just the ambience for gazing.

For a long while nothing happened and I thought that it would not work out that evening. My luck however was in and slowly the scene began coming alive and I saw awesome scenes of battle and bloodshed come alive on the wall before me. As these battles continued Maya came out of a corner of the scenario wearing a hill dress and ceremonial collar. I was entranced immediately and almost prostrated myself before her. I restrained myself and waited for her to speak.

' You have more or less completed your work here, and should be planning on going back. Keep in mind that it is important for you to meditate, to gaze and to chant the mantra that I have given you. With the help of these three you will go by any and every trial that you will be put to by life. So don't be despondent. I have come to you a little while before you go back so that you have the time to enjoy the snows for one last time which perhaps will never happen again to you. The plains will swallow you up and you will go back and find your salvation there. A very special place will however remain in your mind for the mountains and especially the snows. Who knows one day you return to live here at the end of your days. I do not however see such possibilities in your life since the fact of the matter is that you are a desi and not a pahari. As such your primary allegiances are to the plains and the plains folks. Yet for all that you have made good friends here, who unfortunately are in the older age group. By the time you think of coming back they will all be gone to the other world. Kaptan doesn't have many years to live and Devagiri will not be the same without him, at least for you. So enjoy yourself with your friends and head back. Take some rest and get on with your work. Remember the great gods and myself watch on all those who have a keen interest in spirituality. We will not deny you victory, and not just once, but time and time again'. Maya's face looked pensive but not for long and she flashed me her brilliant smile, and I felt the burden of having to depart for the plains melt away from me and my heart was once again at peace.

'I want you to go back now and I am quite sure that I will not be able to come back to stay at a long stretch like this one. Moreover I don't want to come back in this way where my stay is cut short by extraneous circumstances, and there are dark clouds of work looming in the horizon. Indeed all this spoils the enjoyment to a large extent. I pray to you Maya that the next time it happens for me it should be a stretch that has no definite end whether it is in these mountains or elsewhere.' I was getting nostalgic.

'It cannot be these mountains, and it cannot be Devagiri. Your time in Devagiri is over, but there are other mountains that will beckon you and welcome you. Don't worry about that, it will all be taken care of. Now rest and wind up your work and take a bus back to Delhi'. Maya was showing a concern that was beyond the usual. In fact she was not her normal flippant self at all. I sensed that something was wrong and that I should probe that possibility with her.

'Is something the matter? Are you hiding something from me?" I asked in a sudden sensation of doom.

' Don't worry, my friend ', said Maya ' it will all end up well, but the return to civilization is not going to be too easy for you, and it was this that I was hinting at. You will find yourself a stranger in a world that doesn't care for the values of the mountains in the way that you do. You may not be a pahari by birth but you have adopted much of their sensitivity and values. It will take a few weeks before you will be roadworthy. Don't worry, just rest will put you through the worst period and then, once again on with the work'. Maya was serious and even dismayed.

'Thanks for the intimation, and I sincerely believe that I need a good rest, let alone a good haircut and shave, and some nutritious food. I will do as you say and wind up my work here and get back to Delhi '. I was distraught as I knew myself that fitting into the straitjacket of life in the capital of India Delhi would take an effort. The freedom of the mountains was just not there. Nevertheless there was the anonymity of the large metropolitan and that was a big compensation. I ended the gazing session after thanking Maya and taking my leave of her and promising her that I would get in touch with her as soon as I could in Delhi.

After about a month I gathered my possessions and left for Delhi. I had managed to get in touch with my parents and they had come to the distant cantonment where I had reached myself. After a few days there where it was bitterly cold we left by road for Delhi and into the lap of the plains which were to see the next part of my struggle through life. I was glad to be leaving and to be with my parents again. My outer self was already transformed and I no longer wore the long hair and beard that I had grown in Devagiri. I was fully aware that I was in need of rest and looked forward to it.

With this I end the allegorical account of my spiritual journey in the mountains with several holy men and hidden spiritual masters. The journey that followed this one was not so specifically to do with one or the other spiritual masters but the teachings of these men and how they sustained me through my life. With this I take leave of my reader and express the hope that this sojourn together with me was a happy, pleasant, and instructive one, and that given the opportunity I would be able to continue with my narrative of what happened after I got back to the plains !

PART THREE

Afterword

The proper field for allegorical sociology is in folklore, myths, and epic mythology, all of which are told, retold and reshaped as time goes by. Some of these are enacted on stage and film and are the basic bloc of the belief systems and psychological patterns of society. What is more important is that they have an interdisciplinary approach and this is reflected in overall concerns to provide socialization and basic education to all the members of the society.

The mentioned areas of narrative have a deep allegorical content which makes it possible for the impossible to take part in the cultural imprinting of the tender human mind. That such imprinting takes place at a young age and is reiterated well into the adult years, even unto very old age. Thus fabula and epic mythology become a bridge between the individual minds of society and provide a common basis for morality and popular ideology. Thus the members of all societies and nation states that members of all societies and nation states owe a common allegiance owe common allegiance to the state because they have been groomed from birth to do precisely this.

Two of the most versatile allegorical accounts of social relationships and the various sociological theories, are the Ramayana and the Mahabharata. We are not concerned with retelling of the story line or the structure of the allegories, but in pointing out through them several universal facts:

1. Epics, mythology, and allegorical narratives go far beyond the constraints of the usual social science;
2. Unlike social science texts of the present age they tend to accrete over time; that is new elements and accounts tend to be inserted into them either in writing or representations on the stage where the allegorical remains intact;
3. Allegorical narratives, no matter what their form and structure have a vast impact on the human mind and it is seldom noticed that the accretions in story line proceed unobstructed and are in fact welcomed "silently";
4. Allegorical reality or unreality can only be experienced but it's impact cannot be proved or disproved historically speaking;
5. Allegorical writing is based on the assumption that it is bound to comment upon morals and values, rather than stake a claim for the reality or unreality of the narrative;
6. The principle characters and events imbibe in the experiencer a "global" mindset.

These points can be exemplified by a sharp look at some of the aspects of the Ramayana, and the Mahabharata. Both these epic allegories were written well before the Christian era commenced.

The Ramayana and it's morality begin on a dramatic note when the King suddenly orders his eldest son, Ram to go into exile for 14 years, just as he is preparing for a monarchical reign. The justification provided for this shocking directive by the King as being the result of the fulfillment of a boon he had owed one of his queens.

The eldest son Ram goes into forest exile and is accompanied by his younger brother and his young wife who refuses categorically to be parted from Ram, as this is part of her duty, just as Ram's decision to go into exile is a major aspect of filial duty, which insists on complete obedience to the father and mother.

The epic allegory relates many adventures of Ram during exile in the forests. However a most dramatic turn occurs when Sita, wife of Ram is abducted by a stratagem, by the Demon King Ravana.

Following many adventures and allegorical turns of fate, the allies of Ram, the Maruts or "monkey people" decide to help Ram recover Sita, who was being held captive in a beautiful garden surrounded by deep water. She had refused to cooperate in any way with the Demon King Ravana. After many trials and tribulations Hanuman the monkey-god devotee of Ram and a powerful chieftain in his own right, rescues Sita.

Here the allegory could have ended very satisfactorily. However the 'allegorical imperative" does not allow this to happen. The entire epic is meant to transmit morals and values and the rescue of Sita sets the stage for a great deal of symbolic reflections on the story of Ram and Sita. Thus the "allegorical imperative" comes into being, which leads further to the propounding of deep philosophy. Some of the most complex questions are raised and some indications of a solution are also explored. Thus Ram begins to suspect Sita's "purity", or sexual fidelity in its widest ramifications, after their successful return from exile and Ram's triumphant assumption of Kingship.

Unable to accept Sita's assurances that she is completely innocent, Ram arranges an "ordeal by fire" in which Sita has to enter when it is blazing. If she is burnt to death she is guilty, and if not burnt to death she is proved "innocent". Sita successfully clears her character by not being scathed by the fire when she steps into it as it blazes.

However now the allegory turns on to further

complex issues, depicting the character of the ultimate man and woman and their relationship if they were made king and queen. The ruled subjects are however still not satisfied by Sita going succesfully through the "ordeal by fire", and Ram as king has to satisfy the subjects by exiling Sita into a forest hermitage where she gives birth to twins. Meanwhile Ram rules the Kingdom with a golden life size statue of Sita seated next to his own throne.

This is the bare outline of Ram's story, which is a masterpiece allegory. The entire plot is workable on the 'plausibility principle'. The 'plausibility principle' is applicable to all allegorical writing. Thus if were to begin questioning this principle, the very reason for the allegorical account would fail -there are too many unanswered questions and reactions from the main characters, are wholly paradoxical.

Thus when Ram's father asks him to abandon the kingdom and go into exile, what would the 'normal' reaction have been? The normal reaction would have been to refuse to obey such an unfair order. Why should Ram be made a party to the promises given by his father to one of his queens ? Why does he agree to go into exile, what is his fault? How is it that the people of the Kingdom, who swear by Ram, do not revolt against this most whimsical suggestion of Ram's father?

Moreover the character of 'woman' is depicted as being both 'good' and 'bad'. Till the point of abduction by the Demon-King Sita is depicted as an 'ideal' woman who is wholly devoted to her spouse. However after she is rescued from the clutches of Ravana the suspicious nature of Ram and the necessity of letting the people's will prevail in the Kingdom forces Ram to act as an 'ideal' King, whose accountability is totally to the people who are being governed. These are some of the paradoxes, which have to be 'smoothed over' through the "plausibility principle".

The sage who first wrote the epic also had in mind the observance of 'filial piety' and wanted to stress 'obedience to the father' as an ultimate cardinal principle. No matter how these values are stressed in theory and discourse they cannot be as effective as when put across allegorically. Thus the Ramayana consistently takes an allegorical stand. In the narrative we have ample demonstration of the allegorical imperative, replete with talking and intelligent animals, magical transformations, animals with superhuman powers, paradoxes, and so on.

Therefore allegorical writing including mythology takes as its point of departure a particular value or moral principle, which is dramatized and introduced in a way that it, is ultimately plausible. Thus the backbone of allegory of any sort, especially allegorical sociological accounts is that the events described could be possible and cannot be completely ruled out. This is very important because right behind the 'plausibility principle' lies the overt/covert 'didacticism principle.' Thus the oneness with nature, the magical forest, the virtues of selflessness, and the communion with flora and fauna are all extolled in the Ramayana, which is enacted every year on stage in most parts of India and many parts of south-east Asia. Thus allegorical writing is a tool for teaching purposes, in the realm of spirituality. Since the spirit ultimately knows no cages or boundaries the narrative in allegory is most imaginative. In sociological allegories we are not overly concerned with trying to be realistic. In allegory the word 'impossible' does not exist, either in theory or in practice.

All is possible in an allegory, and the writer is expected to practice 'artistic license' to use incidents in such a way that it in defiance of all rules of logic. This is what makes allegorical writing a spiritually uplifting didactic creation.

Another masterpiece of allegorical writing in India is the Mahabharata, which itself antedates the Christian era, but was written some time later than the Ramayana. The Mahabharata abounds in allegorical themes built around political quest for power. In this allegory the 'good' Pandavas enter into a dice game with the 'evil' Kauravas. In this dice game the gambling goes on until the Pandavas stake everything even their common wife. They lose everything.

The Kauravas order Draupadi, common wife of the Pandavas, to be disrobed in front of the assembly. In a magnificent allegorical act Sri Krishna, God-Incarnate makes the sari worn by Draupadi of infinite length and the Kauravas are unable to further humiliate the Pandavas and Draupadi in particular. The Pandavas are sent in exile and have many adventures, and then return to take back their kingdom as had been agreed upon, and become ruling princes again. The Kauravas refuse to part with even a small village, let alone the Kingdom. This was a blatant breach of trust and led directly to the Great War or the Mahabharata. On the battle field of Kurukshetra Sri Krishna gives sage advice to Arjun the archer regarding life and death. This segment is called the 'Bhagavad-Gita'. The Gita is an accretion to the earlier version, but by now it has become virtually the 'heart' of the text. In the Gita the immortality of the soul is extolled at the very outset. Several spiritual methods are presented and explored for the realization of the Self. Ultimately it is stressed that faith in the deity is the key to peace of mind and it is advocated that actions to be pure have to be without motive or selfish purposes.

The armies take up their position on opposite ends of the battleground. In the preamble to the hostilities the main archer of the Pandavas breaks down in front of Sri Krishna his charioteer and claims he doesn't want to get into an internecine situation, where he is found guilty of attacking and killing relatives and teachers. There could be no more allegorical an insertion of a sacred text than the Gita when the two opposed armies are about to blow the bugle and commence the war.

Thus once we accept this allegorical insertion the text becomes autonetic in a very powerful way. It begins to affect the psyche of the reader or viewer, and questions of implausibility are set aside, and do not matter.

The Gita was adjoined to the Mahabharata some hundreds of years after the story had been accreted. Yet the Gita section in itself is hugely allegorical assuming clairvoyance, clairaudience, mystic visions and even the revelation of the Ultimate Effulgence. Whether any of the characters of the Ramayana or the Mahabharata, ever existed or were modelled on someone, remains a matter for speculation. What is not controversial is the fact that the Gita has wonderful insights to offer anyone willing to read it carefully with due reflection. This is didactic spirituality, so central to any allegorical excursion.

We have been talking about allegoricism in the pre-Christian era. However this form of communication was not abandoned in ancient times. We find in the middle ages/ medieval times a vast host of allegorical writings emerged. During these times various versions of the Bible and Quran and Upanishads were compiled and their message of spirituality was disseminated in a mix of historical narrative and allegory. In fact the parables and teachings of allegoricism give it an immense capacity to communicate to the widest possible audience.

What at first appears to be a simple story/parable

makes great moral impact when pondered upon. The point of the miracles of Jesus, like 'walking on water' and making the blind 'see' are undoubtedly allegorical. The reality/unreality of miracles and parables is hardly worth speculation. The reality is discovered only in meditation or deep thought. Yet if such miracles are allegorical so also is the sermon on the Mount, as preached by Jesus. From a high mound Jesus discoursed and fed a huge crowd from food within a basket that never emptied. Thus spiritual discourse can never be removed from allegory and serves the purpose of making a life story of the spiritual personages, masters, or saints into figures, which are far removed from the common ilk.

There is another factor, which often bypasses the intellect. Each great allegory leaves a stamp on the common consciousness of mankind as a whole. Each allegorical account influences the style and content of the stories, which follow such creations.

Over time the allegorical contents of the teachings become the moral backbone of a renewed spirituality and often enunciate a new religion. Part of the spiritual allegory of great masters is an allegorical prophecy that they will incarnate again and continue to enunciate their teachings. The masters promise to help their followers by their spiritual powers from even beyond the grave when they are no longer physically present. It is oftern indicated in their prophecies that they will return in a physical self at some appointed moment in time. Such is the power of prophecies of return that they enthuse entirely new generations of followers waiting for the master to incarnate and put the world right. This has however often led to problematics, such as blind faith in the teacher. In recent times such blind faith in the spiritual teacher has led to prophecies of doom and catastrophe. These in turn have sometimes triggered off 'mass suicide' in recent times. However going by the numerical occurrence of such extreme actions, the number of such catastrophes is relatively negligible. Yet it does indicate that the faith the members of cults have in their chosen master is extreme and usually completely emotional rather than rational.

Spiritual allegories are at one end of the spectrum, and religious diktats are at the other. While all religions of the world form a casing for spirituality, spirituality itself is basically a search for meaning to life, bereft of religious trappings. While spirituality is flexible in approach religion is relatively rigid. No specific religion happens to be free of its trappings such as life cycle rituals, sacrifices, chants, litanies, priests, temples, churches and mosques. Spirituality is an effort on the other hand, to make the adherent forget his mortality and enjoy the bliss of being immortal in soul. Every religion promises, that the faithful adherents to it will be 'saved' after death, and the soul revert to some ideal world like that of Swarga (Hinduism), Heaven (Christianity), and 'Jannat' (Islam).

The hope of an ideal typical utopic abode and the resurrection of the body therein are found in the most ancient religions, as also the most contemporary cults, sects and denominations. This tends to lead the believer into vast areas of endeavour to be good, kind, charitable, affectionate, loving and worshipful. Were the allegorical and ritual contents to be missing from spirituality and religion, even partial peace and order would not be possible. Various religions have sometimes been criticized as being the 'opium' that is used by people to forget pain and sorrow. This is an ambiguous statement. It fails to point out that in the face of a totally theodical life situation the mind of man has to be ordered ideologically for normal survival on a day-to day basis. This alone can help a person to be able to bear the shock of acute grief that comes with death of all types (premature, tragic, violent etc.) of death, unavoidable misfortune, and ultimately old age. If the ideologies of the existing religions did not provide a cushioning effect under circumstances of crisis and grief they would have only superficial effect on the lives of devotees and adherents. In fact religion and spirituality have emerged because there was a need to prevent mankind from falling into a destructive depression whenever something inexplicable happened personally or societally.

Spirituality is the very spine of religion, and if religion is exoteric, then spirituality is esoteric. It is the monks, bhikkhus, sadhus and all those who make meditation a way of life who are responsible for exploring the inner reality of mind and brain through their esoteric practices. Monks often live in monasteries, in small dark rooms to induce the spiritual experience of being one with the universe. This experience of 'oneness' is sought after by the Hindu Sadhus, and the pirs who embody the Sufi tradition. As such what we are dealing with is inward journey into the depths of human consciousness. Thus the spirituality of one religion differs only marginally from that of another. The goal is the same in all of them: total psychological freedom.

Since we are interested in allegorical sociology and the inward journey let us take and discuss an example of the recent paragons in this area. One prime example of spiritual allegory is that of Ramakrishna Paramhans (1836-1886). This is a well documented spiritual hagiography, and is due to the zealous notes taken on Ramakrishna's daily life, by 'M' a disciple of his. 'M' took copious verbatim reports on the everyday life of Ramakrishna and compiled them into a large volume called 'The Gospel of Sri Ramakrishna.' In these verbatim reports Ramakrishna appears to be a metaphor or allegory himself, so out of the ordinary was his daily life.

According to Ramakrishna it is the irresistible lure of wealth on the one hand, and sexual desire on the other that have held mankind in a double bind from which it is very difficult to emerge. Thus in the spiritual teachings of Ramakrishna what stands at the centre of the 'trap' in which the ego of man is caged is the 'impossibility' of giving up those very factors which are the crux of the entanglement of the spirit.

It is found on reflection that an overwhelming majority of mankind is not particularly interested in breaking out of the prison of the ego, which guides mankind towards those very activities, which would generate sensuality of all types. Moreover the drive for wealth and sexuality encases almost evey other facet of existence. So far as acquisition of wealth is concerned it is at the root of the quest for political and social power. It is not possible that political power is present without the support of and actual expenditure of wealth. This in turn creates a base for influencing people and their actions. The wealthy and the powerful use their already strong entrenchment in society to satisfy their sensual whims and to pursue wealth further. There is no limit to the wealth that a man or a collectivity can aspire to. The acquisition of wealth goes automatically to produce a deep desire to accumulate greater wealth, as it is the base from which sensual desires can be temporarily satisfied and the ego stroked and stoked. Thus 'woman' in this parlance is used generically by Ramakrishna as a rubric for all craving of the senses. It is not possible to wish these desires away as they are both inbred physically and psychologically in the existence of mankind. The desire to go beyond the senses is not a major force in the life of most people. To ask a person to abndon the use of the senses to satisfaction would be a futile endeavor. However this position as adopted by Ramakrishna in his teachings implies that the proper and dutiful use of the senses is necessary to keep the physical body from rebelling and developing the ego further rather that paring it down to a manageable condition. The ancient scriptures prescribe that the senses be given their due but that the devotee does not get embedded in them. Hence this stance of Ramakrishna is essentially allegorical in that ' woman and gold' become symbols rather than the reality to what they are pointing towards (social and psychic reality).

The central theme of Ramakrishna's teaching, which we are discussing, does not come alive if we take the pointers literally. The major accent is upon the social and psychological metamorphosis of the entire field of the senses and ontological craving for power through the medium of capital consolidation. Thus when we refer to 'woman', the communication does not refer to the female of the species alone. Were it so then it would be clear that the teaching has been left half interpreted and therefore essentially incomplete. Thus would it be possible for us to say that the problem of existence hinges around theme of 'man and gold'. In contemporary times the persistent gender wars indicate that 'woman' cannot be singled out and once again provide a male chauvinistic philosophy. Thus this usage (woman and gold) has already become dated and it is time that it is clarified that what is being referred to is the domain of sensuality and not the female of the species. The teaching applies equally to man and woman on a human scale.

Why is it that Ramakrishna warns against the trap of the senses and their ability to capture the mind and intellect of men and women ? This is because the human body works through signals sent to the brain from all its constituent parts. Of these centres of sensuality it can easily be said that the reproductive centres are extremely powerful and demanding. Right from the beginning of life they begin to work towards perpetuating the human race. It is all right to use sensuality and sexuality within a "marital" frame, yet this is scarcely done. Once the senses have become used to a particular sensual experience they tend to become addicted and obsessed with gaining vast variety in such experience. As these experiences are repeated there emanated an obsession and acute enthusiasm to further widen the repertoire of experience.

There is a sense of incompleteness if the senses do not hold sway over a person. And further no matter how polished the exterior of aperson, within he or she is a cauldron of sensual desire. Ramakrishna warned against this kind of dominion of the senses over the mind and the intellect. It was not his intention to vilify the female gender but to indicate that any form of obsessive desire would lead a person to abandoning himself to sensual fulfillment.

Is this really a block on the spiritual path? Our answer has to do with the fact that sensuality leads to deployment of energy in the sensual domain and it becomes the main goal for the practitioner. It is primarily a lack of spiritual and intellectual energy, which has plagued mankind through the ages. There is no sufficient energy to devote to the holistic spectrum of living and man becomes enervated to a great extent. It is this loss of energy in sensual pursuits rather than spiritual goals, which leads to the wide range of frustrations that ultimately create relationships which are superficial and conflictual, leading even to the breakup of marital ties. Thus the conquest of sensuality would by itself lead to a world in which there is mutual care and consideration. The occurrence of all manner of bloodshed is an indicator that the mind of man has become embedded in the ego. Allegorical accounts by symbolizing this condition attempt to overcome it and are in this sense the domain of the pursuit of inner peace of mind and spirit.

In the account given above (The Hindu Journey) it is clear that the narrative is interdisciplinary and allegorical. As such we must let the text communictate in itself and by itself. Reading the text is therefore the best way to get a feel of allegoricism and how it creates the expansion of the overall scope of sociology and the social sciences.

BIBLIOGRAPHY

Brown , R 1973 : *A First Language : early stages.Cambridge,* Mass : Harvard University Press.

Clekley, H. 1955 : The Mask of Sanity. St. Louis : Mosby

Durkheim, E, 1926 : *The Elementary Forms of The Religious Life.* London : Allen and Unwin.

Evans-Pritchard, E.E. 1937 : *Witchcraft,·Oracles and Magic Among the Azande.* London : Oxford University Press.

Evans-Pritchard, E.E. 1940 : *The Nuer.* : Oxford. Clarendon Press.

Goffman, E. 1959. : *The presentation of self in every day life.* Garden city. N.Y. : Doubleday.

Goffman E., 1963 : *Behaviour in Public places : notes on the social organization of gatherings.* New York : The Free Press Mills, *The Sociological Imagination.* New York : Oxford University Press. C. W. 1959 :

Menninger, K. 1942 : *The Human Mind*. New York: Knopf Radcliffe Brown, A.R. 1948 : *The Andaman Islanders*. Glencoe, Ill.

Sudnow, D. 1967. : *Passing On : The social organization of dying*. Englewood Cliffs, N.J. : Prentice. Hall Weber, M. 1958. *The Religion of India . Glencoe, Ill. the Free Press.*

Wittgenstein, L. 1953 : *Philosophical Investigations*. New York: The Macmillan Co.

Index

L

M

O

P

R

S